ENGLISH AND SCOTTISH

BALLADS.

EDITED BY

FRANCIS JAMES CHILD.

VOLUME VI.

BOSTON:

LITTLE, BROWN AND COMPANY.

M.DCCC.LX.

RIVERSIDE, CAMBRIDGE:
STEREOTYPED AND PRINTED BY
H. O. HOUGHTON AND COMPANY.

CONTENTS OF VOLUME SIXTH.

BOOK VI.

BOOK VI.

THE LOCHMABEN HARPER.

THIS fine old ballad was first printed in the *Musical Museum* (*O heard ye e'er of a silly blind Harper*, p. 598). Scott inserted a different copy, equally good, in the *Border Minstrelsy*, i. 422, and there is another, of very ordinary merits, in *Scottish Traditional Versions of Ancient Ballads* (*The Jolly Harper*), p. 37. In this the theft is done on a wager, and the booty duly restored. On account of the excellence of the ballad, we give two versions, though they differ but slightly.

O HEARD ye of a silly Harper,
  Liv'd long in Lochmaben town,
How he did gang to fair England,
  To steal King Henry's Wanton Brown?

But first he gaed to his gude wife
  Wi' a' the speed that he coud thole:
"This wark," quo' he, "will never work,
  Without a mare that has a foal."

Quo' she, "Thou hast a gude grey mare,
That'll rin o'er hills baith low and hie;
Gae tak' the grey mare in thy hand,
And leave the foal at hame wi' me.

"And tak a halter in thy hose,
And o' thy purpose dinna fail;
But wap it o'er the Wanton's nose;
And tie her to the grey mare's tail:

"Syne ca' her out at yon back yeate,
O'er moss and muir and ilka dale,
For she'll ne'er let the Wanton bite,
Till she come hame to her ain foal."

So he is up to England gane,
Even as fast as he can hie,
Till he came to King Henry's yeate;
And wha' was there but King Henry?

"Come in," quo' he, "thou silly blind Harper,
And of thy harping let me hear;"
"O, by my sooth," quo' the silly blind Harper,
"I'd rather hae stabling for my mare."

The King looks o'er his left shoulder,
And says unto his stable groom,
"Gae tak the silly poor Harper's mare,
And tie her 'side my wanton brown."

And ay he harpit, and ay he carpit,
  Till a' the lords gaed through the floor;
They thought the music was sae sweet,
  That they forgat the stable door.

And ay he harpit, and ay he carpit,
  Till a' the nobles were sound asleep,
Than quietly he took aff his shoon,
  And saftly down the stair did creep.

Syne to the stable door he hies,
  Wi' tread as light as light coud be,
And whan he open'd and gaed in,
  There he fand thirty good steeds and three.

He took the halter frae his hose,
  And of his purpose did na' fail;
He slipt it o'er the Wanton's nose,
  And tied it to his grey mare's tail.

He ca'd her out at yon back yeate,
  O'er moss and muir and ilka dale,
And she loot ne'er the Wanton bite,
  But held her still gaun at her tail.

The grey mare was right swift o' fit,
  And did na fail to find the way,
For she was at Lochmaben yeate,
  Fu' lang three hours ere it was day.

When she came to the Harper's door,
  There she gae mony a nicher and snear;
"Rise," quo' the wife, "thou lazy lass,
  Let in thy master and his mare."

Then up she raise, pat on her claes,
  And lookit out through the lock hole;
"O, by my sooth," then quoth the lass,
  "Our mare has gotten a braw big foal."

"Come haud thy peace, thou foolish lass,
  The moon's but glancing in thy ee,
I'll wad my haill fee 'gainst a groat,
  It's bigger than e'er our foal will be."

The neighbours too that heard the noise
  Cried to the wife to put her in;
"By my sooth," then quoth the wife,
  "She's better than ever he rade on."

But on the morn at fair day light,
  When they had ended a' their chear,
King Henry's Wanton Brown was stawn,
  And eke the poor old Harper's mare.

"Alace! alace!" says the silly blind Harper,
  "Alace! alace! that I came here,
In Scotland I've tint a braw cowte foal,
  In England they've stawn my guid grey mare."

"Come had thy tongue, thou silly blind Harper,
  And of thy alacing let me be,
For thou shall get a better mare,
  And weel paid shall thy cowte foal be."

LOCHMABEN HARPER.

Minstrelsy of the Scottish Border, i. 422.

O HEARD ye na o' the silly blind Harper,
  How long he lived in Lochmaben town?
And how he wad gang to fair England,
  To steal the Lord Warden's Wanton Brown?

But first he gaed to his gude wyfe,
  Wi' a the haste that he could thole—
"This wark," quo' he, "will ne'er gae weel,
  Without a mare that has a foal."

Quo' she—"Thou hast a gude gray mare,
  That can baith lance o'er laigh and hie;
Sae set thee on the gray mare's back,
  And leave the foal at hame wi' me."

So he is up to England gane,
  And even as fast as he may drie;
And when he cam to Carlisle gate,
  O whae was there but the Warden hie?

"Come into my hall, thou silly blind Harper,
And of thy harping let me hear!"
"O, by my sooth," quo' the silly blind Harper,
"I wad rather hae stabling for my mare."

The Warden look'd ower his left shoulder,
And said unto his stable groom—
"Gae take the silly blind Harper's mare,
And tie her beside my Wanton Brown."

Then aye he harped, and aye he carped,
Till a' the lordlings footed the floor;
But an the music was sae sweet,
The groom had nae mind o' the stable door.

And aye he harped, and aye he carped,
Till a' the nobles were fast asleep;
Then quickly he took aff his shoon,
And saftly down the stair did creep.

Syne to the stable door he hied,
Wi' tread as light as light could be;
And when he open'd and gaed in,
There he fand thirty steeds and three.

He took a cowt halter frae his hose,
And o' his purpose he didna fail;
He slipt it ower the Wanton's nose,
And tied it to his gray mare's tail.

He turn'd them loose at the castle gate,
  Ower muir and moss and ilka dale;
And she ne'er let the Wanton bait,
  But kept him a-galloping hame to her foal.

The mare she was right swift o' foot,
  She didna fail to find the way;
For she was at Lochmaben gate
  A lang three hours before the day.

When she came to the Harper's door,
  There she gave mony a nicker and sneer—
"Rise up," quo' the wife, "thou lazy lass;
  Let in thy master and his mare."

Then up she rose, put on her clothes,
  And keekit through at the lock-hole—
"O, by my sooth," then cried the lass,
  "Our mare has gotten a braw brown foal!"

"Come haud thy tongue, thou silly wench!
  The morn's but glancing in your ee;
I'll wad my hail fee against a groat,
  He's bigger than e'er our foal will be."

Now all this while in merry Carlisle
  The Harper harped to hie and law,
And the fiend dought they do but listen him to,
  Until that the day began to daw.

But on the morn at fair daylight,
  When they had ended a' their cheer,
Behold the Wanton Brown was gane,
  And eke the poor blind Harper's mare!

"Allace! allace!" quo' the cunning auld Harper,
  "And ever allace that I cam here;
In Scotland I hae lost a braw cowt foal,
  In England they've stown my gude gray mare!"

"Come, cease thy allacing, thou silly blind Harper,
  And again of thy harping let us hear;
And weel payd sall thy cowt-foal be,
  And thou sall have a far better mare."

Then aye he harped, and aye he carped,
  Sae sweet were the harpings he let them hear!
He was paid for the foal he had never lost,
  And three times ower for the gude Gray Mare.

JOHNIE OF BREADISLEE.

AN ANCIENT NITHSDALE BALLAD.

Minstrelsy of the Scottish Border, iii. 114.

"THE hero of this ballad appears to have been an outlaw and deer-stealer—probably one of the broken men residing upon the Border. There are several different copies, in one of which the principal personage is called *Johnie of Cockielaw.* The stanzas of greatest merit have been selected from each copy. It is sometimes said, that this outlaw possessed the old Castle of Morton, in Dumfries-shire, now ruinous: "Near to this castle there was a park, built by Sir Thomas Randolph, on the face of a very great and high hill; so artificially, that, by the advantage of the hill, all wild beasts, such as deers, harts, and roes, and hares, did easily leap in, but could not get out again; and if any other cattle, such as cows, sheep, or goats, did voluntarily leap in, or were forced to do it, *it is doubted* if their owners were permitted to get them out again." *Account of Presbytery of Penpont, apud Macfarlane's MSS.* Such a park would form a convenient domain to an outlaw's castle, and the mention of Durisdeer, a neighboring parish, adds weight to this tradition."

Johnie of Breadislee was first printed in the *Border Minstrelsy.* Fragments of two other versions, in which the hero's name is Johny Cock, were given in Fry's *Pieces of Ancient Poetry*, Bristol, 1814, p. 55, and the editor did not fail to notice that he had probably lighted on the ballad of *Johny Cox*, which Ritson says the Rev. Mr. Boyd faintly recollected, (*Scottish Song*, I. p. xxxvi.) Motherwell, not aware of what Fry had done, printed a few stanzas belonging to the first of these versions, under the title of *Johnie of Braidisbank* (*Minstrelsy, Ancient and Modern*, p. 23), and Kinloch recovered a nearly complete story. Another copy of this last has been published from Buchan's manuscripts in *Scottish Traditional Versions of Ancient Ballads* (Percy Society, vol. xvii. p. 77). Chambers, in his *Scottish Ballads*, p. 181, has compounded Scott's, Kinloch's, and Motherwell's copies, interspersing a few additional stanzas of no value. Scott's and Kinloch's versions are given in this place, and Fry's fragments (which contain several beautiful stanzas) in the Appendix.

JOHNIE rose up in a May morning,
Call'd for water to wash his hands—
"Gar loose to me the gude graie dogs,
That are bound wi' iron bands."

When Johnie's mother gat word o' that,
Her hands for dule she wrang—
"O Johnie! for my benison,
To the greenwood dinna gang!

"Eneugh ye hae o' gude wheat bread,
And eneugh o' the blood-red wine;
And, therefore, for nae venison, Johnie,
I pray ye, stir frae hame."

But Johnie's busk't up his gude bend bow,
  His arrows, ane by ane,
And he has gane to Durrisdeer,
  To hunt the dun deer down.

As he came down by Merriemass,
  And in by the benty line,
There has he espied a deer lying
  Aneath a bush of ling.

Johnie he shot, and the dun deer lap,
  And he wounded her on the side;
But atween the water and the brae,
  His hounds they laid her pride.

And Johnie has bryttled the deer sae weel,
  That he's had out her liver and lungs;
And wi' these he has feasted his bluidy hounds,
  As if they had been earl's sons.

They eat sae much o' the venison,
  And drank sae much o' the blude,
That Johnie and a' his bluidy hounds
  Fell asleep as they had been dead.

And by there came a silly auld carle,
  An ill death mote he die!
For he's awa' to Hislinton,
  Where the Seven Foresters did lie.

"What news, what news, ye gray-headed carle,
  What news bring ye to me?"
"I bring nae news," said the gray-headed carle,
  "Save what these eyes did see.

"As I came down by Merriemass,
  And down among the scroggs,
The bonniest childe that ever I saw
  Lay sleeping amang his dogs.

"The shirt that was upon his back
  Was o' the Holland fine;
The doublet which was over that
  Was o' the Lincome twine.

"The buttons that were on his sleeve
  Were o' the goud sae gude:
The gude graie hounds he lay amang,
  Their mouths were dyed wi' blude."

Then out and spak the First Forester,
  The heid man ower them a'—
"If this be Johnie o' Breadislee,
  Nae nearer will we draw."

But up and spak the Sixth Forester,
  (His sister's son was he,)
"If this be Johnie o' Breadislee,
  We soon shall gar him die!"

The first flight of arrows the Foresters shot,
They wounded him on the knee;
And out and spak the Seventh Forester,
" The next will gar him die."

Johnie's set his back against an aik,
His fute against a stane;
And he has slain the Seven Foresters,
He has slain them a' but ane.

He has broke three ribs in that ane's side,
But and his collar bane;
He's laid him twa-fald ower his steed,
Bade him carry the tidings hame.

" O is there nae a bonnie bird
Can sing as I can say,
Could flee away to my mother's bower,
And tell to fetch Johnie away?"

The starling flew to his mother's window stane,
It whistled and it sang;
And aye the ower word o' the tune
Was—" Johnie tarries lang!"

They made a rod o' the hazel bush,
Another o' the slae-thorn tree,
And mony mony were the men
At fetching o'er Johnie.

Then out and spake his auld mother,
And fast her tears did fa'—
"Ye wad nae be warn'd, my son Johnie,
Frae the hunting to bide awa'.

"Aft hae I brought to Breadislee
The less gear and the mair,
But I ne'er brought to Breadislee
What grieved my heart sae sair.

"But wae betyde that silly auld carle!
An ill death shall he die!
For the highest tree in Merriemas
Shall be his morning's fee."

Now Johnie's gude bend bow is broke,
And his gude graie dogs are slain;
And his bodie lies dead in Durrisdeer,
And his hunting it is done.

JOHNIE OF COCKLESMUIR.

From Kinloch's *Ancient Scottish Ballads*, p. 38. This version was procured in the North Country. The termination would seem to be wanting, for the story must have had a tragical conclusion. Buchan's copy ends very insipidly with the King's granting Johny a free license to hunt!

Johnie rose up in a May morning,
  Call'd for water to wash his hands;
And he has call'd for his gude gray hunds,
  That lay bund in iron bands, *bands,*
  That lay bund in iron bands.

" Ye'll busk, ye'll busk my noble dogs,
  Ye'll busk and mak them boun,
For I'm going to the Broadspear-hill,
  To ding the dun deer doun, *doun,* &c.

Whan Johnie's mither heard o' this,
  She til her son has gane—
" Ye'll win your mither's benison,
  Gin ye wad stay at hame.

" Your meat sall be of the very very best,
  And your drink o' the finest wine;
And ye will win your mither's benison,
  Gin ye wad stay at hame."

His mither's counsel he wad na tak,
  Nor wad he stay at hame;
But he's on to the Broadspear-hill,
  To ding the dun deer doun.

Johnie lookit east, and Johnie lookit west,
  And a little below the sun;
And there he spied the dun deer sleeping,
  Aneath a buss o' brume.

Johnie shot, and the dun deer lap,
And he's woundit him in the side;
And atween the water and the wud
He laid the dun deer's pride.

They ate sae meikle o' the venison,
And drank sae meikle o' the blude,
That Johnie and his twa gray hunds,
Fell asleep in yonder wud.

By there cam a silly auld man,
And a silly auld man was he;
And he's aff to the proud foresters,
To tell what he did see.

"What news, what news, my silly auld man,
What news? come tell to me;"
"Na news, na news," said the silly auld man,
"But what my een did see.

"As I cam in by yon greenwud,
And doun amang the scrogs,
The bonniest youth that e'er I saw,
Lay sleeping atween twa dogs.

"The sark that he had on his back,
Was o' the Holland sma';
And the coat that he had on his back,
Was laced wi' gowd fu' braw."

Up bespak the first forester,
The first forester of a'—
"And this be Johnie o' Cocklesmuir,
It's time we were awa."

Up bespak the niest forester,
The niest forester of a'—
"And this be Johnie Cocklesmuir,
To him we winna draw."

The first shot that they did shoot,
They woundit him on the thie;
Up bespak the uncle's son,—
"The niest will gar him die."

"Stand stout, stand stout, my noble dogs,
Stand stout and dinna flee;
Stand fast, stand fast, my gude gray hunds,
And we will mak them die."

He has killed six o' the proud foresters,
And wounded the seventh sair;
He laid his leg out owre his steed,
Says, "I will kill na mair."

THE SANG OF THE OUTLAW MURRAY.

Minstrelsy of the Scottish Border, i. 369.

"THIS ballad appears to have been composed about the reign of James V. It commemorates a transaction supposed to have taken place betwixt a Scottish monarch and an ancestor of the ancient family of Murray of Philiphaugh, in Selkirkshire. The Editor is unable to ascertain the historical foundation of the tale; nor is it probable that any light can be thrown upon the subject, without an accurate examination of the family charter-chest. . . . .

"The merit of this beautiful old tale, it is thought, will be fully acknowledged. It has been, for ages, a popular song in Selkirkshire. The scene is by the common people supposed to have been the Castle of Newark upon Yarrow. This is highly improbable, because Newark was always a royal fortress. Indeed, the late excellent antiquarian, Mr. Plummer, Sheriff-depute of Selkirkshire, has assured the Editor that he remembered the *insignia* of the unicorns, &c., so often mentioned in the ballad, in existence upon the old Tower of Hangingshaw, the seat of the Philiphaugh family; although, upon first perusing a copy of the ballad, he was inclined to subscribe to the popular opinion. The Tower of Hangingshaw has been demolished for many years. It stood in a romantic and solitary situation, on the classical banks of the Yarrow. When the mountains around Hangingshaw were covered with the wild copse which constituted a Scottish forest, a more secure stronghold for an outlawed baron can scarcely be imagined.

"The tradition of Ettrick Forest bears, that the outlaw was a man of prodigious strength, possessing a baton or club, with which he laid *lee* (*i. e.* waste) the country for many miles round; and that he was at length slain by Buccleuch, or some of his clan, at a little mount, covered with fir-trees, adjoining to Newark Castle, and said to have been a part of the garden. A varying tradition bears the place of his death to have been near to the house of the Duke of Buccleuch's gamekeeper, beneath the castle; and that the fatal arrow was shot by Scott of Haining, from the ruins of a cottage on the opposite side of Yarrow. There were extant, within these twenty years, some verses of a song on his death. The feud betwixt the Outlaw and the Scots, may serve to explain the asperity with which the chieftain of that clan is handled in the ballad.

"In publishing the following ballad, the copy principally resorted to is one apparently of considerable antiquity, which was found among the papers of the late Mrs. Cockburn of Edinburgh, a lady whose memory will be long honoured by all who knew her. Another copy, much more imperfect, is to be found in Glenriddel's MSS. The names are in this last miserably mangled, as is always the case when ballads are taken down from the recitation of persons living at a distance from the scenes in which they are laid. Mr. Plummer also gave the editor a few additional verses, not contained in either copy, which are thrown into what seemed their proper place. There is yet another copy in Mr. Herd's MSS., which has been occasionally made use of. Two verses are restored in the present edition, from the recitation of Mr. Mungo Park, whose toils during his patient and intrepid travels in Africa have not eradicated from his recollection the legendary lore of his native country."—S.

Since the above was printed, Mr. Aytoun has published still another copy of this piece, (*Ballads of Scotland*, ii. 129,) from a manuscript in the Philiphaugh charter-chest. I cannot assent to the praise bestowed by Scott on *The Outlaw Murray*. The story lacks point, and the style is affected—not that of the unconscious poet of the real *traditional* ballad.

ETTRICKE FORESTE is a feir foreste,
In it grows manie a semelie trie;
There's hart and hynd, and dae and rae,
And of a' wilde bestis grete plentie.

There's a feir castelle, bigged wi' lyme and stane;
O gin it stands not pleasauntlie!
In the fore front o' that castelle feir,
Twa unicorns are bra' to see:

There's the picture of a knight, and a ladye bright,
And the grene hollin abune their brie:
There an Outlaw kepis five hundred men,
He keepis a royalle cumpanie.

His merryemen are a' in ae liverye clad,
O' the Lincome grene sae gaye to see;
He and his ladye in purple clad,
O gin they lived not royallie!

Word is gane to our nobil King,
  In Edinburgh where that he lay,
That there was an Outlaw in Ettricke Foreste,
  Counted him nought, nor a' his courtrie gay.

"I make a vowe," then the gude King said,
  "Unto the man that deir bought me,
I'se either be King of Ettricke Foreste,
  Or King of Scotlande that Outlaw sall be!"

Then spake the lord hight Hamilton,
  And to the nobil King said he,
"My sovereign prince, sum counsell take,
  First at your nobilis, syne at me.

"I redd ye, send yon braw Outlaw till,
  And see gif your man cum will he:
Desyre him cum and be your man,
  And hald of you yon Foreste frie.

"Gif he refuses to do that,
  We'll conquess baith his landis and he!
Or else, we'll throw his castell down,
  And make a widowe o' his gaye ladye."

The King then call'd a gentleman,
  James Boyd (the Earle of Arran his brother [was he);

38. Thomas Boyd, Earl of Arran, was forfeited, with his father and uncle, in 1469, for an attempt on the person of James III. He had a son, James, who was restored, and in favor with James IV. about 1482. If this be the person here

When James he cam before the King,
He knelit befor him on his knè.

"Wellcum, James Boyd!" said our nobil King,
"A message ye maun gang for me;
Ye maun hye to Ettricke Foreste,
To yon Outlaw, where bydeth he.

"Ask him of whom he haldis his landis,
Or man, wha may his master be,
And desyre him cum, and be my man,
And hald of me yon Foreste frie.

"To Edinburgh to cum and gang,
His safe warrant I sall gie;
And gif he refuses to do that,
We'll conquess baith his landis and he.

"Thou mayst vow I'll cast his castell down,
And mak a widowe o' his gaye ladye;
I'll hang his merryemen, payr by payr,
In ony frith where I may them see."

James Boyd tuik his leave o' the nobil King,
To Ettricke Foreste feir cam he;
Down Birkendale Brae when that he cam,
He saw the feir Foreste wi' his ee.

meant, we should read, "The Earl of Arran his *son* was he." Glenriddel's copy reads, "a Highland laird I'm sure was he." Reciters sometimes call the messenger the Laird of Skene.—S.

60. Birkendale Brae, now commonly called *Birkendailly*, is

Baith dae and rae, and harte and hinde,
And of a' wilde bestis great plentie;
He heard the bows that bauldly ring,
And arrows whidderan' hym near bi.

Of that feir castell he got a sight;
The like he neir saw wi' his ee!
On the fore front o' that castell feir,
Twa unicorns were gaye to see;
The picture of a knight, and ladye bright,
And the grene hollin abune their brie.

Thereat he spyed five hundred men,
Shuting with bows on Newark Lee;
They were a' in ae livery clad,
O' the Lincome grene sae gaye to see.

His men were a' clad in the grene,
The knight was armed capapie,
With a bended bow, on a milk-white steed,
And I wot they rank'd right bonnilie:
Thereby Boyd kend he was master man,
And served him in his ain degré.

63, Scott, *blows:* Aytoun, *bows.*

a steep descent on the south side of Minch-moor, which separates Tweeddale from Ettrick Forest; and from the top of which we have the first view of the woods of Hangingshaw, the Castle of Newark, and the romantic dale of Yarrow.—S.

"God mot thee save, brave Outlaw Murray!
Thy ladye, and all thy chyvalrie!"
"Marry, thou's wellcum, gentleman,
Some king's messenger thou seemis to be."

"The King of Scotlonde sent me here,
And, gude Outlaw, I am sent to thee;
I wad wot of whom ye hald your landis,
Or man, wha may thy master be?"

"Thir landis are MINE!" the Outlaw said;
"I ken nae king in Christentie;
Frae Soudron I this foreste wan,
When the King nor his knightis were not to see."

"He desyres you'l cum to Edinburgh,
And hauld of him this foreste fre;
And, gif ye refuse to do this,
He'll conquess baith thy landis and thee.
He hath vow'd to cast thy castell down,
And mak a widowe o' thy gaye ladye;

"He'll hang thy merryemen, payr by payr,
In ony frith where he may them finde."
"Ay, by my troth!" the Outlaw said,
"Than wauld I thinke me far behinde.

"Ere the King my feir countrie get,
This land that's nativest to me,

Mony o' his nobilis sall be cauld,
  Their ladyes sall be right wearie."

Then spak his ladye, feir of face,
  She seyd, "Without consent of me,
That an Outlaw suld come befor a King;
  I am right rad of treasonrie.
Bid him be gude to his lordis at hame,
  For Edinburgh my lord sall nevir see."

James Boyd tuik his leave o' the Outlaw kene,
  To Edinburgh boun is he;
When James he cam before the King,
  He knelit lowlie on his kné.

"Welcum, James Boyd!" seyd our nobil King;
  "What foreste is Ettricke Foreste frie?"
"Ettricke Foreste is the feirest foreste
  That evir man saw wi' his ee.

"There's the dae, the rae, the hart, the hynde,
  And of a' wild bestis grete plentie;
There's a pretty castell of lyme and stane,
  O gif it standis not pleasauntlie!

"There's in the fore front o' that castell,
  Twa unicorns, sae bra' to see;
There's the picture of a knight, and a ladye bright,
  Wi' the grene hollin abune their brie.

"There the Outlaw keepis five hundred men,
He keepis a royalle cumpanie;
His merryemen in ae livery clad,
O' the Lincome grene sae gaye to see:
He and his ladye in purple clad;
O gin they live not royallie!

"He says, yon foreste is his awin;
He wan it frae the Southronie;
Sae as he wan it, sae will he keep it,
Contrair all kingis in Christentie."

"Gar warn me Perthshire, and Angus baith,
Fife, up and downe, and Louthians three,
And graith my horse!" said our nobil King,
"For to Ettricke Forest hie will I me."

Then word is gane the Outlaw till,
In Ettricke Forest, where dwelleth he,
That the King was cuming to his cuntrie,
To conquess baith his landis and he.

"I mak a vow," the Outlaw said,
"I mak a vow, and that trulie,
Were there but three men to tak my pairt,
Yon King's cuming full deir suld be!"

Then messengers he called forth,
And bade them hie them speedilye—

"Ane of ye gae to Halliday,
The Laird of the Corehead is he.

"He certain is my sister's son;
Bid him cum quick and succour me!
The King cums on for Ettricke Foreste,
And landless men we a' will be."

"What news? What news?" said Halliday,
"Man, frae thy master unto me?"
"Not as ye wad; seeking your aide;
The King's his mortal enemie."

"Ay, by my troth!" said Halliday,
"Even for that it repenteth me;
For gif he lose feir Ettricke Foreste,
He'll tak feir Moffatdale frae me.

"I'll meet him wi' five hundred men,
And surely mair, if mae may be;
And before he gets the foreste feir,
We a' will die on Newark Lee!"

The Outlaw call'd a messenger,
And bid him hie him speedilye,
To Andrew Murray of Cockpool,

154. This is a place at the head of Moffat-water, possessed of old by the family of Halliday.—S.

173. This family were ancestors of the Murrays, Earls of Annandale; but the name of the representative, in the time

"That man's a deir cousin to me;
Desyre him cum, and make me aide,
With a' the power that he may be."

"It stands me hard," Andrew Murray said,
"Judge gif it stand na hard wi' me;
To enter against a king wi' crown,
And set my landis in jeopardie!
Yet, if I cum not on the day,
Surely at night he sall me see."

To Sir James Murray of Traquair,
A message came right speedilye—

of James IV., was William, not Andrew. Glenriddel's MS. reads, "the country-keeper."—S.

183. Before the Barony of Traquair became the property of the Stewarts, it belonged to a family of Murrays, afterwards Murrays of Black-barony, and ancestors of Lord Elibank. The old castle was situated on the Tweed. The lands of Traquair were forfeited by Willielmus de Moravia, previous to 1464; for, in that year, a charter, proceeding upon his forfeiture, was granted by the crown to "Willielmo Douglas de Cluny." Sir James was, perhaps, the heir of William Murray. It would farther seem, that the grant in 1464 was not made effectual by Douglas; for another charter from the crown, dated the 3d February, 1478, conveys the estate of Traquair to James Stewart, Earl of Buchan, son of the Black Knight of Lorne, and maternal uncle to James III., from whom is descended the present Earl of Traquair. The first royal grant not being followed by possession, it is very possible that the Murrays may have continued to occupy Traquair long after the date of that charter. Hence, Sir James might have reason to say, as in the ballad, "The King has gifted my lands lang syne."—S.

"What news? What news?" James Murray said,
  "Man, frae thy master unto me?"

"What neids I tell? for weel ye ken
  The King's his mortal enemie;
And now he is cuming to Ettricke Foreste,
  And landless men ye a' will be."

"And, by my trothe," James Murray said,
  "Wi' that Outlaw will I live and die;
The King has gifted my landis lang syne—
  It cannot be nae warse wi' me."

The King was cuming thro' Caddon Ford,
  And full five thousand men was he;
They saw the derke Foreste them before,
  They thought it awsome for to see.

Then spak the lord hight Hamilton,
  And to the nobil King said he,
"My sovereign liege, sum council tak,
  First at your nobilis, syne at me.

"Desyre him mete thee at Permanscore,
  And bring four in his cumpanie;
Five Erles sall gang yoursell befor,
  Gude cause that you suld honour'd be.

195. A ford on the Tweed, at the mouth of the Caddon Burn, near Yair.—S.

"And, gif he refuses to do that,
We'll conquess baith his landis and he;
There sall nevir a Murray, after him,
Hald land in Ettricke Foreste free."

Then spak the kene Laird of Buckscleuth,
A stalworthe man, and sterne was he—
"For a King to gang an Outlaw till,
Is beneath his state and his dignitie.

"The man that wons yon foreste intill,
He lives by reif and felonie!
Wherefore, brayd on, my sovereign liege,
Wi' fire and sword we'll follow thee;
Or, gif your countrie lords fa' back,
Our Borderers sall the onset gie."

Then out and spak the nobil King,
And round him cast a wilie ee—
"Now, had thy tongue, Sir Walter Scott,
Nor speak of reif nor felonie:
For had every honest man his awin kye,
A right puir clan thy name wad be!"

The King then call'd a gentleman,
Royal banner-bearer there was he,
James Hoppringle of Torsonse, by name;
He cam and knelit upon his knè.

"Wellcum, James Pringle of Torsonse!
A message ye maun gang for me:

Ye maun gae to yon Outlaw Murray,
Surely where bauldly bideth he.

"Bid him mete me at Permanscore,
And bring four in his cumpanie;
Five erles sall cum wi' mysell,
Gude reason I suld honour'd be.

"And gif he refuses to do that,
Bid him luke for nae good o' me!
There sall nevir a Murray, after him,
Have land in Ettricke Foreste free."

James cam before the Outlaw kene,
And served him in his ain degré—
"Welcum, James Pringle of Torsonse!
What message frae the King to me?"

"He bids ye meet him at Permanscore,
And bring four in your cumpany;

247. Permanscore is a very remarkable hollow on the top of a high ridge of hills, dividing the vales of Tweed and Yarrow, a little to the eastward of Minch-moor. It is the outermost point of the lands of Broadmeadows. The Glenriddel MS., which, in this instance, is extremely inaccurate as to names, calls the place of rendezvous, "*The Poor Man's House*," and hints that the Outlaw was surprised by the treachery of the King:—

"Then he was aware of the King's coming,
With hundreds three in company,
'I wot the muckle deel * * * * *

Five erles sall gang himsell befor,
  Nae mair in number will he be.

"And gif you refuse to do that,
  (I freely here upgive wi' thee,)
He'll cast yon bonny castle down,
  And make a widowe o' that gay ladye.

" He'll loose yon bluidhound Borderers,
  Wi' fire and sword to follow thee ;
There will nevir a Murray, after thysell,
  Have land in Ettrick Foreste free."

"It stands me hard," the Outlaw said,
  " Judge gif it stands na hard wi' me,
Wha reck not losing of mysell,
  But a' my offspring after me.

" My merryemen's lives, my widowe's teirs—
  There lies the pang that pinches me ;
When I am straught in bluidie eard,
  Yon castell will be right dreirie.

He learned Kingis to lie!
  For to fetch me here frae amang my men,
Here, like a dog for to die.' "

I believe the reader will think with me, that the catastrophe is better, as now printed from Mrs. Cockburn's copy. The deceit, supposed to be practised on the Outlaw, is unworthy of the military monarch, as he is painted in the ballad; especially if we admit him to be King James IV. —S.

"Auld Halliday, young Halliday,
Ye sall be twa to gang wi' me;
Andrew Murray, and Sir James Murray,
We'll be nae mae in cumpanie."

When that they cam before the King,
They fell before him on their kné—
"Grant mercie, mercie, nobil King!
E'en for his sake that dyed on tree."

"Sicken like mercie sall ye have,
On gallows ye sall hangit be!"
"Over God's forbode," quoth the Outlaw then,
"I hope your grace will bettir be;
Else, ere you come to Edinburgh port,
I trow thin guarded sall ye be.

"Thir landis of Ettricke Foreste fair,
I wan them from the enemie;
Like as I wan them, sae will I keep them,
Contrair a' kingis in Christentie."

All the nobilis the King about,
Said pitie it were to see him dee—
"Yet grant me mercie, sovereign prince,
Extend your favour unto me!

"I'll give thee the keys of my castell,
Wi' the blessing o' my gay ladye,
Gin thou'lt make me sheriffe of this Foreste,
And a' my offspring after me."

" Wilt thou give me the keys of thy castell,
Wi' the blessing of thy gaye ladye?
I'se make thee sheriffe of Ettricke Foreste,
Surely while upward grows the tree;
If you be not traitour to the King,
Forfaulted sall thou nevir be."

" But, Prince, what sall cum o' my men?
When I gae back, traitour they'll ca' me.
I had rather lose my life and land,
Ere my merryemen rebuked me."

" Will your merryemen amend their lives,
And a' their pardons I grant thee?
Now, name thy landis where'er they lie,
And here I RENDER them to thee."—

" Fair Philiphaugh is mine by right,
And Lewinshope still mine shall be;
Newark, Foulshiells, and Tinnies baith,
My bow and arrow purchased me.

"And I have native steads to me,
The Newark Lee and Hanginshaw;

312. In this and the following verse, the ceremony of feudal investiture is supposed to be gone through, by the Outlaw resigning his possessions into the hands of the king, and receiving them back, to be held of him as superior. The lands of Philiphaugh are still possessed by the Outlaw's representative. Hangingshaw and Lewinshope were sold of late years. Newark, Foulshiels, and Tinnies, have long belonged to the family of Buccleuch.—S.

I have mony steads in the forest schaw,
But them by name I dinna knaw."

The keys of the castell he gave the King,
Wi' the blessing o' his feir ladye;
He was made sheriffe of Ettricke Foreste,
Surely while upward grows the tree;
And if he was na traitour to the King,
Forfaulted he suld never be.

Wha ever heard, in ony times,
Sicken an outlaw in his degré,
Sic favour get befor a King,
As did the OUTLAW MURRAY of the Foreste
free?

JOHNIE ARMSTRANG.

"JOHNIE ARMSTRONG, of Gilnockie, the hero of the following ballad, is a noted personage, both in history and tradition. He was, it would seem from the ballad, a brother of the Laird of Mangertoun, chief of the name. His place of residence (now a roofless tower) was at the Hollows, a few miles from Langholm, where its ruins still serve to adorn a scene, which, in natural beauty, has few equals in Scotland. At the head of a desperate band of freebooters, this Armstrong is said to have spread the terror of his name almost as far as Newcastle, and to have levied black-mail, or protection and forbearance money, for many miles round. James V., of whom it was long remembered by his grateful people that he made the "rush-bush keep the cow," about 1529, undertook an expedition through the Border counties, to suppress the turbulent spirit of the Marchmen. But before setting out upon his journey, he took the precaution of imprisoning the different Border chieftains, who were the chief protectors of the marauders. The Earl of Bothwell was forfeited, and confined in Edinburgh Castle. The Lords of Home and Maxwell, the Lairds of Buccleuch, Fairniherst, and Johnston, with many others, were also committed to ward. Cockburn of Henderland, and Adam Scott of Tushielaw, called the King of the Border, were publicly executed. —LESLEY, p. 430. The King then marched rapidly forward, at the head of a flying army of ten thousand men, through Ettrick Forest and Ewsdale. The evil genius of our Johnie Armstrong, or, as others say, the private advice of some courtiers, prompted him to present himself before James, at the head of thirty-six horse, arrayed in all the pomp of Border chivalry. Pitscottie uses nearly the words of the ballad, in describing the splendor of his equipment, and his high expectations of favor from the King. "But James, looking upon him sternly, said to his attendants, 'What wants that knave that a king should have?' and ordered him and his followers to instant execution."—"But John Armstrong," continues this minute historian, "made great offers to the King: That he should sustain himself, with forty gentlemen, ever ready at his service, on their own cost, without wronging any Scottishman: Secondly, that there was not a subject in England, duke, earl, or baron, but, within a certain day, he should bring him to his majesty, either quick or dead. At length, he seeing no hope of favor, said very proudly, 'It is folly to seek grace at a graceless face; but,' said he, 'had I known this, I should have lived upon the Borders in despite of King Harry and you both; for I know King Harry would *downweigh my best horse with gold*, to know that I were condemned to die this day."—PITSCOTTIE'S *History*, p. 145. Johnie and all his retinue were accordingly hanged upon growing trees, at a place called Carlenrig Chapel, about ten miles above Hawick, on the high road to Langholm. The country people believe, that, to manifest the injustice of the execution, the trees withered away. Armstrong and his followers were buried in a deserted churchyard, where their graves are still shown.

"As this Border hero was a person of great note in his way, he is frequently alluded to by the writers of the time. Sir David Lindsay of the Mount, in the curious play published by Mr. Pinkerton, from the Bannatyne MS., introduces a pardoner, or knavish dealer in relics, who produces, among his holy rarities—

—— " The cordis, baith grit and lang,
Quhilk hangit Johnnie Armstrang,
Of gud hempt, soft and sound.
Gud haly pepill, I stand ford,
Quhavir beis hangit in this cord,
Neidis nevir to be dround!"

PINKERTON'S *Scottish Poems*, vol. ii. p. 69.

"In *The Complaynt of Scotland*, John Armistrangis' dance, mentioned as a popular tune, has probably some reference to our hero." [See the *Musical Museum*, ed. 1853, vol. iv. p. 336.]—SCOTT'S *Minstrelsy*, i. 402.

The ballad as here given is to be found in *A Collection of Old Ballads*, 1723, vol. i. p. 170. The whole title is: *Johnny Armstrang's Last Good-night, shewing how John Armstrong, with his eightscore men, fought a bloody battle with the Scotch King at Edenborough.* It had previously appeared in *Wit Restor'd*, 1658, p. 123, in very good shape, except the want of some stanzas towards the end. It is in this form, says Motherwell, that the story is preserved in the mouths of the people. Nevertheless, Allan Ramsay has inserted in his *Evergreen* quite a different version, taken down from the mouth of a gentleman of the name of Armstrong, "the sixth generation from this John," which the reciter maintained to be the genuine ballad, "and the common one false."

Ramsay's copy is subjoined, and the imperfect edition from *Wit Restor'd* finds a place in the Appendix.

The following verses, generally styled *Armstrong's Good-night*, are said to have been composed by one of that tribe who was executed in 1601 for the murder of Sir John Carmichael, Warden of the Middle Marches. They are from Johnson's *Museum*, p. 620, and are also found in Herd's *Scottish Songs*, ii. 182. In Buchan's *Ballads of the North of Scotland*, ii. 127, there is a twaddling piece called *The Last Guid Night*, which is a sort of imitation of these stanzas.

The night is my departing night,
  The morn's the day I maun awa,
There's no a friend or fae of mine,
  But wishes that I were awa.

What I hae done for lack o' wit
  I never never can reca';
I trust ye're a' my friends as yet,
  Gude night, and joy be wi' you a'.

Is there ever a man in all Scotland,
  From the highest estate to the lowest degree,
That can shew himself now before our King?
  Scotland is so full of treachery.

Yes, there is a man in Westmorland,
  And Johnny Armstrong they do him call;
He has no lands nor rents coming in,
  Yet he keeps eightscore men within his hall.

He has horses and harness for them all,
  And goodly steeds that be milk-white,
With their goodly belts about their necks,
  With hats and feathers all alike.

The King he writes a loving letter,
  And with his own hand so tenderly,
And hath sent it unto Johnny Armstrong,
  To come and speak with him speedily.

When John he look'd this letter upon,
  He lok'd as blith as a bird in a tree;
"I was never before a King in my life,
  My father, my grandfather, nor none of us three.

"But seeing we must go before the King,
Lord, we will go most gallantly;
Ye shall every one have a velvet coat,
Laid down with golden laces three.

"And every one shall have a scarlet cloak,
Laid down with silver laces five,
With your golden belts about your necks,
With hats and feathers all alike."

But when Johnny went from Giltnock-Hall,
The wind it blew hard, and full fast it did rain;
"Now fare thee well, thou Giltnock-Hall,
I fear I shall never see thee again."

Now Johnny he is to Edenborough gone,
With his eightscore men so gallantly,
And every one of them on a milk-white steed,
With their bucklers and swords hanging to their knee.

But when John came the King before,
With his eightscore men so gallant to see,
The King he mov'd his bonnet to him,
He thought he had been a king as well as he.

"O pardon, pardon, my sovereign liege,
Pardon for my eightscore men and me;
For my name, it is Johnny Armstrong,
And subject of yours, my liege," said he.

"Away with thee, thou false traytor,
No pardon will I grant to thee,
But to-morrow morning by eight of the clock,
I will hang up thy eightscore men and thee."

Then Johnny look'd over his left shoulder,
And to his merry men thus said he,
"I have asked grace of a graceless face,
No pardon there is for you and me."

Then John pull'd out his good broad sword,
That was made of the mettle so free;
Had not the King moved his foot as he did,
John had taken his head from his fair body.

"Come, follow me, my merry men all,
We will scorn one foot for to fly;
It shall never be said we were hang'd like dogs;
We will fight it out most manfully."

Then they fought on like champions bold,
For their hearts were sturdy, stout, and free;
'Till they had kill'd all the King's good guard,—
There were none left alive but one, two, or three.

But then rose up all Edenborough,
They rose up by thousands three;
A cowardly Scot came John behind,
And run him through the fair body.

Said John, "Fight on, my merry men all,
I am a little wounded, but am not slain;
I will lay me down to bleed a while,
Then I'll rise and fight with you again."

Then they fought on like mad men all,
Till many a man lay dead on the plain,
For they were resolved before they would yield,
That every man would there be slain.

So there they fought couragiously,
'Till most of them lay dead there and slain,
But little Musgrave, that was his foot-page,
With his bonny Grissel got away unta'n.

But when he came to Giltnock-Hall,
The Lady spy'd him presently;
"What news, what news, thou little foot-page,
What news from thy master, and his company?"

"My news is bad, Lady," he said,
"Which I do bring, as you may see,
My master Johnny Armstrong is slain,
And all his gallant company.

"Yet thou are welcome home, my bonny Grissel,
Full oft thou hast been fed with corn and hay,
But now thou shalt be fed with bread and wine,
And thy sides shall be spurr'd no more, I say."

O then bespake his little son,
  As he sat on his nurse's knee,
"If ever I live to be a man,
  My father's death reveng'd shall be."

JOHNIE ARMSTRANG.

From Ramsay's *Evergreen*, ii. 190.

SUM speiks of lords, sum speiks of lairds,
  And sicklike men of hie degrie;
Of a gentleman I sing a sang,
  Sumtyme calld Laird of Gilnockie.

The King he wrytes a luving letter,
  With his ain hand sae tenderly,
And he hath sent it to Johny Armstrang,
  To cum and speik with him speidily.

The Elliots and Armstrangs did convene,
  They were a gallant company—
"We'il ryde and meit our lawfull King,
  And bring him safe to Gilnockie.

"Make kinnen and capon ready, then,
  And venison in great plenty;
We'il welcome hame our royal King;
  I hope he'il dyne at Gilnockie!"

They ran their horse on the Langholme howm,
  And brake their speirs with mekle main;
The ladys lukit frae their loft windows—
  "God bring our men weil back again!"

When Johny came before the King,
  With all his men so brave to see,
The King he movit his bonnet to him;
  He wein'd he was a King as well as he.

"May I find grace, my sovereign liege,
  Grace for my loyal men and me?
For my name it is Johny Armstrang,
  And subject of yours, my liege," said he.

"Away, away, thou traytor strang!
  Out of my sicht sune mayst thou be!
I grantit nevir a traytors lyfe,
  And now I'll not begin with thee."

"Grant me my lyfe, my liege, my King!
  And a bonny gift I will give to thee—
Full four-and-twenty milk-whyt steids,
  Were a' foald in a yeir to me.

"I'll gie thee all these milk-whyt steids,
  That prance and nicher at a speir;
With as mekle gude Inglis gilt,
  As four of their braid backs dow beir."

17. Langum hown. 30. thou mayst sune.

"Away, away, thou traytor strang!
  Out o' my sicht sune mayst thou be!
I grantit nevir a traytors lyfe,
  And now I'll not begin with thee!"

"Grant me my lyfe, my liege, my King!
  And a bonny gift I'll gie to thee—
Gude four-and-twenty ganging mills,
  That gang throw a' the yeir to me.

"These four-and-twenty mills complete
  Sall gang for thee throw all the yeir;
And as mekle of gude reid wheit,
  As all thair happers dow to bear."

"Away, away, thou traytor strang!
  Out o' my sicht sune mayst thou be!
I grantit nevir a traytors lyfe,
  And now I'll not begin with thee."

"Grant me my lyfe, my liege, my King!
  And a great gift I'll gie to thee—
Bauld four-and-twenty sisters' sons,
  Sall for thee fecht, tho all sould flee!"

"Away, away, thou traytor strang!
  Out o' my sicht sune mayst thou be!
I grantit nevir a traytors lyfe,
  And now I'll not begin with thee."

"Grant me my lyfe, my liege, my King!
And a brave gift I'll gie to thee—
All betwene heir and Newcastle town
Sall pay their yeirly rent to thee."

"Away, away, thou traytor strang!
Out o' my sicht sune mayst thou be!
I grantit nevir a traytors lyfe,
And now I'll not begin with thee."

"Ye lied, ye lied, now, King," he says,
"Althocht a king and prince ye be!
For I luid naithing in all my lyfe,
I dare well say it, but honesty—

"But a fat horse, and a fair woman,
Twa bonny dogs to kill a deir;
But Ingland suld haif found me meil and malt,
Gif I had livd this hundred yeir!

"Scho suld haif found me meil and malt,
And beif and mutton in all plentie;
But neir a Scots wyfe could haif said,
That eir I skaithd her a pure flie.

"To seik het water beneth cauld yce,
Surely it is a great folie;
I haif asked grace at a graceles face,
But there is nane for my men and me!

"But had I kend, or I came frae hame,
  How thou unkind wadst bene to me,
I wad haif kept the Border syde,
  In spyte of all thy force and thee.

"Wist Englands King that I was tane,
  O gin a blyth man wald he be!
For anes I slew his sisters son,
  And on his breist-bane brak a tree."

John wore a girdle about his midle,
  Imbroidred owre with burning gold,
Bespangled wi' the same mettle
  Maist beautifull was to behold.

Ther hang nine targats at Johnys hat,
  And ilka an worth three hundred pound—
"What wants that knave that a King suld haif,
  But the sword of honour and the crown?

"O whair gat thou these targats, Johnie,
  That blink sae brawly abune thy brie?"
"I gat them in the field fechting,
  Wher, cruel King, thou durst not be.

"Had I my horse, and harness gude,
  And ryding as I wont to be,
It sould haif bene tald this hundred yeir,
  The meiting of my King and me!

"God be withee, Kirsty, my brither,
Lang live thou Laird of Mangertoun!
Lang mayst thou live on the Border syde,
Or thou se thy brither ryde up and doun.

"And God be withee, Kirsty, my son,
Whair thou sits on thy nursees knee!
But and thou live this hundred yeir,
Thy fathers better thou'lt never be.

Farweil, my bonny Gilnock-Hall,
Whair on Esk syde thou standest stout!
Gif I had leived but seven yeirs mair,
I wald haif gilt thee round about."

John murdred was at Carlinrigg,
And all his galant companie;
But Scotlands heart was never sae wae,
To see sae mony brave men die.

Because they savd their country deir
Frae Englishmen: nane were sae bauld,
Whyle Johnie livd on the Border syde,
Nane of them durst cum neir his hald.

HUGHIE GRAHAM.

Of the two editions of this ballad which follow, the first is taken from *The Scots Musical Museum* (p. 312), to which it was contributed by Burns. Burns states that he obtained his copy from oral tradition in Ayrshire, but he had certainly retouched several stanzas (the ninth and tenth, says Cromek), and the third and eighth are entirely of his composition.

The other copy is from the *Border Minstrelsy*, and consists of a version "long current in Selkirkshire" (procured for Scott by Mr. William Laidlaw), which also has been slightly improved by the pen of the editor.

In the Appendix we have placed the story as it occurs in Durfey's *Pills to purge Melancholy*, and in Ritson's *Ancient Songs*. The seventeenth volume of the Percy Society Publications furnishes us with a Scottish version in which Sir Hugh is rescued and sent over the sea: *Scottish Traditional Versions of Ancient Ballads*, p. 73. These, we believe, are all the published forms of this ballad, unless we mention Mr. Allan Cunningham's *réchauffé* of Burns, in his *Songs of Scotland*, i. 327.

"According to *tradition*," says Mr. Stenhouse, "Robert Aldridge, Bishop of Carlisle, about the year 1560, seduced the wife of Hugh Graham, one of those bold and predatory chiefs who so long inhabited what was called the Debatable Land, on the English and

Scottish border. Graham, being unable to bring so powerful a prelate to justice, in revenge made an excursion into Cumberland, and carried off *inter alia*, a fine mare belonging to the bishop (!) but being closely pursued by Sir John Scroope, warden of Carlisle, with a party on horseback, was apprehended near Solway Moss, and carried to Carlisle, where he was tried and convicted of felony. Great intercessions were made to save his life; but the bishop, it is said, being determined to remove the chief obstacle to his guilty passions, remained inexorable, and poor Graham fell a victim to his own indiscretion and his wife's infidelity. Anthony Wood observes that there were many changes in this prelate's time, both in church and state, but that he retained his offices and preferments during them all."—*Musical Museum*, iv. 297.

OUR lords are to the mountains gane,
A hunting o' the fallow deer,
And they hae gripet Hughie Graham,
For stealing o' the Bishop's mare.

And they hae tied him hand and foot,
And led him up thro' Stirling town;
The lads and lasses met him there,
Cried, "Hughie Graham, thou art a loun."

"O lowse my right hand free," he says,
"And put my braid sword in the same,
He's no in Stirling town this day,
Daur tell the tale to Hughie Graham."

Up then bespake the brave Whitefoord,
As he sat by the bishop's knee,
"Five hundred white stots I'll gie you,
If ye'll let Hughie Graham gae free."

"O haud your tongue," the bishop says,
"And wi' your pleading let me be;
For tho' ten Grahams were in his coat,
Hughie Graham this day shall die."

Up then bespake the fair Whitefoord,
As she sat by the bishop's knee;
"Five hundred white pence I'll gie you,
If ye'll gie Hughie Graham to me."

"O haud your tongue now, lady fair,
And wi' your pleading let it be;
Altho' ten Grahams were in his coat,
It's for my honour he maun die."

They've taen him to the gallows knowe,
He looked to the gallows tree,
Yet never colour left his cheek,
Nor ever did he blin' his e'e.

At length he looked round about,
To see whatever he could spy,
And there he saw his auld father,
And he was weeping bitterly.

"O haud your tongue, my father dear.
And wi' your weeping let it be;
Thy weeping's sairer on my heart,
Than a' that they can do to me.

"And ye may gie my brother John
My sword that's bent in the middle clear,
And let him come at twelve o'clock,
And see me pay the bishop's mare.

"And ye may gie my brother James
My sword that's bent in the middle brown,
And bid him come at four o'clock,
And see his brother Hugh cut down.

"Remember me to Maggy, my wife,
The niest time ye gang o'er the moor;
Tell her, she staw the bishop's mare,
Tell her, she was the bishop's whore.

"And ye may tell my kith and kin
I never did disgrace their blood,
And when they meet the bishop's cloak,
To mak it shorter by the hood."

HUGHIE THE GRÆME.

From *Minstrelsy of the Scottish Border*, iii. 110.

GUDE Lord Scroope's to the hunting gane,
He has ridden o'er moss and muir;
And he has grippet Hughie the Græme,
For stealing o' the Bishop's mare.

"Now, good Lord Scroope, this may not be!
Here hangs a broadsword by my side;
And if that thou canst conquer me,
The matter it may soon be tryed."

"I ne'er was afraid of a traitor thief;
Although thy name be Hughie the Græme,
"I'll make thee repent thee of thy deeds,
If God but grant me life and time."

"Then do your worst now, good Lord Scroope,
And deal your blows as hard as you can;
It shall be tried within an hour,
Which of us two is the better man."

But as they were dealing their blows so free,
And both so bloody at the time,
Over the moss came ten yeomen so tall,
All for to take brave Hughie the Græme.

Then they hae grippit Hughie the Græme,
And brought him up through Carlisle town ;
The lasses and lads stood on the walls,
Crying, "Hughie the Græme, thou'se ne'er gae down !"

Then they hae chosen a jury of men,
The best that were in Carlisle town;
And twelve of them cried out at once,
"Hughie the Græme, thou must gae down!"

Then up bespak him gude Lord Hume,
As he sat by the judge's knee,
"Twenty white owsen, my gude lord,
If you'll grant Hughie the Græme to me."

"O no, O no, my gude Lord Hume,
Forsooth and sae it mauna be;
For were there but three Græmes of the name,
They suld be hanged a' for me."

'Twas up and spake the gude Lady Hume,
As she sat by the judge's knee,
"A peck of white pennies, my good lord judge,
If you'll grant Hughie the Græme to me."

"O no, O no, my gude Lady Hume,
Forsooth and so it must na be;
Were he but the one Græme of the name,
He suld be hanged high for me."

"If I be guilty," said Hughie the Græme,
"Of me my friends shall have small talk;"
And he has louped fifteen feet and three,
Though his hands they were tied behind his back.

He looked over his left shoulder,
And for to see what he might see;
There was he aware of his auld father,
Came tearing his hair most piteouslie.

"O hald your tongue, my father," he says,
"And see that ye dinna weep for me!
For they may ravish me o' my life,
But they canna banish me fro' Heaven hie.

"Fair ye weel, fair Maggie, my wife!
The last time we came ower the muir,
'Twas thou bereft me of my life,
And wi' the Bishop thou play'd the whore.

"Here, Johnie Armstrang, take thou my sword,
That is made o' the metal sae fine;
And when thou comest to the English side,
Remember the death of Hughie the Græme."

KINMONT WILLIE.

In the year 1596, Mr. Salkeld, the deputy of Lord Scroope, the English warden of the West Marches, and Robert Scott, the representative of the Laird of Buccleuch, then keeper of Liddesdale, held a meeting on the border line of the kingdoms, according to the custom of the times, for the purpose of arranging such differences, and redressing such grievances, as either party might have to allege. On these occasions a truce was always proclaimed, inviolable on pain of death, from the day of the meeting to the next day at sunrise. After the conference in question, as William Armstrong of Kinmonth, a notorious freebooter, whose ordinary style was Kinmont Willie, was returning to his home, accompanied by only three or four persons, he was pursued by a couple of hundred Englishmen, taken prisoner, and in contravention of the truce, lodged in the castle of Carlisle. The Laird of Buccleuch sought to obtain the enfranchisement of his client and retainer, through the mediation, first of the English warden, and then of the Scottish ambassador. Receiving no satisfaction, he took the matter into his own hands, raised a party of two hundred horse, surprised the castle of Carlisle, and carried off the prisoner by main force. This dashing achievement was performed on the 13th of April, 1596.

According to a rhymester who celebrated the daring feat of Buccleuch about a hundred years later, Kinmont Willie was a descendant of Johnie Armstrong of Gilnockie.

Interesting details of the surprise of the castle, and further notices of Kinmont Willie are given by Scott in the *Border Minstrelsy* (ii. 32), where the ballad was first published.

"This ballad is preserved," says Scott, "on the West Borders, but much mangled by reciters, so that some conjectural emendations have been absolutely necessary to render it intelligible."

O HAVE ye na heard o' the fause Sakelde?
  O have ye na heard o' the keen Lord Scroope?
How they hae ta'en bauld Kinmont Willie,
  On Haribee to hang him up?

Had Willie had but twenty men,
  But twenty men as stout as he,
Fause Sakelde had never the Kinmont ta'en,
  Wi' eight score in his cumpanie.

They band his legs beneath the steed,
  They tied his hands behind his back;
They guarded him, fivesome on each side,
  And they brought him ower the Liddel-rack.

They led him thro' the Liddel-rack,
  And also thro' the Carlisle sands;
They brought him to Carlisle castell,
  To be at my Lord Scroope's commands.

4. Haribee is the place of execution at Carlisle.—S.
13. The Liddel-rack is a ford on the Liddel.—S.

"My hands are tied, but my tongue is free,
And whae will dare this deed avow?
Or answer by the Border law?
Or answer to the bauld Buccleuch?"

"Now haud thy tongue, thou rank reiver!
There's never a Scot shall set thee free:
Before ye cross my castle yate,
I trow ye shall take farewell o' me."

"Fear na ye that, my lord," quo' Willie:
"By the faith o' my body, Lord Scroope," he said,
"I never yet lodged in a hostelrie,
But I paid my lawing before I gaed."

Now word is gane to the bauld Keeper,
In Branksome Ha' where that he lay,
That Lord Scroope has ta'en the Kinmont Willie,
Between the hours of night and day.

He has ta'en the table wi' his hand,
He garr'd the red wine spring on hie—
"Now Christ's curse on my head," he said,
"But avenged of Lord Scroope I'll be!

"O is my basnet a widow's curch?
Or my lance a wand of the willow-tree?
Or my arm a ladye's lilye hand,
That an English lord should lightly me!

"And have they ta'en him, Kinmont Willie,
  Against the truce of Border tide,
And forgotten that the bauld Buccleuch
  Is keeper here on the Scottish side?

"And have they e'en ta'en him, Kinmont Willie,
  Withouten either dread or fear,
And forgotten that the bauld Buccleuch
  Can back a steed, or shake a spear?

"O were there war between the lands,
  As well I wot that there is none,
I would slight Carlisle castell high,
  Though it were builded of marble stone.

"I would set that castell in a low,
  And sloken it with English blood!
There's never a man in Cumberland,
  Should ken where Carlisle castell stood.

"But since nae war's between the lands,
  And there is peace, and peace should be;
I'll neither harm English lad or lass,
  And yet the Kinmont freed shall be!"

He has call'd him forty Marchmen bauld,
  I trow they were of his ain name,
Except Sir Gilbert Elliot, call'd
  The Laird of Stobs, I mean the same.

He has call'd him forty Marchmen bauld,
Were kinsmen to the bauld Buccleuch;
With spur on heel, and splent on spauld,
And gleuves of green, and feathers blue.

There were five and five before them a',
Wi' hunting-horns and bugles bright:
And five and five came wi' Buccleuch,
Like warden's men, array'd for fight.

And five and five, like a mason gang,
That carried the ladders lang and hie;
And five and five, like broken men;
And so they reach'd the Woodhouselee.

And as we cross'd the Bateable Land,
When to the English side we held,
The first o' men that we met wi',
Whae sould it be but fause Sakelde?

"Where be ye gaun, ye hunters keen?"
Quo' fause Sakelde; "come tell to me!"
"We go to hunt an English stag,
Has trespass'd on the Scots countrie."

"Where be ye gaun, ye marshal men?"
Quo' fause Sakelde; "come tell me true!"

76. A house on the Border, belonging to Buccleuch.—S.

"We go to catch a rank reiver,
  Has broken faith wi' the bauld Buccleuch."

"Where are ye gaun, ye mason lads,
  Wi' a' your ladders lang and hie?"
"We gang to herry a corbie's nest,
  That wons not far frae Woodhouselee."

"Where be ye gaun, ye broken men?"
  Quo' fause Sakelde; "come tell to me!"
Now Dickie of Dryhope led that band,
  And the nevir a word of lear had he.

"Why trespass ye on the English side?
  Row-footed outlaws, stand!" quo' he;
The nevir a word had Dickie to say,
  Sae he thrust the lance through his fause bodie.

Then on we held for Carlisle toun,
  And at Staneshaw-bank the Eden we cross'd;
The water was great and meikle of spait,
  But the nevir a horse nor man we lost.

And when we reach'd the Staneshaw-bank,
  The wind was rising loud and hie;
And there the Laird garr'd leave our steeds,
  For fear that they should stamp and nie.

102. Eden has been substituted for Eske, the latter name being inconsistent with geography.—S.

And when we left the Staneshaw-bank,
  The wind began full loud to blaw ;
But 'twas wind and weet, and fire and sleet,
  When we came beneath the castle wa'.

We crept on knees, and held our breath,
  Till we placed the ladders against the wa' ;
And sae ready was Buccleuch himsell
  To mount the first before us a'.

He has ta'en the watchman by the throat,
  He flung him down upon the lead—
" Had there not been peace between our lands,
  Upon the other side thou hadst gaed !

" Now sound out, trumpets ! " quo' Buccleuch ;
  " Let's waken Lord Scroope right merrilie ! "
Then loud the warden's trumpet blew—
  O wha dare meddle wi' me ?

Then speedilie to wark we gaed,
  And raised the slogan ane and a',
And cut a hole through a sheet of lead,
  And so we wan to the castle ha'.

They thought King James and a' his men
  Had won the house wi' bow and spear ;
It was but twenty Scots and ten,
  That put a thousand in sic a stear!

124. The name of a Border tune.—S.

Wi' coulters, and wi' forehammers,
  We garr'd the bars bang merrilie,
Until we came to the inner prison,
  Where Willie o' Kinmont he did lie.

And when we cam to the lower prison,
  Where Willie o' Kinmont he did lie—
"O sleep ye, wake ye, Kinmont Willie,
  Upon the morn that thou's to die?"

"O I sleep saft, and I wake aft,
  It's lang since sleeping was fley'd frae me;
Gie my service back to my wife and bairns,
  And a' gude fellows that spier for me."

Then Red Rowan has hente him up,
  The starkest man in Teviotdale—
"Abide, abide now, Red Rowan,
  Till of my Lord Scroope I take farewell.

"Farewell, farewell, my gude Lord Scroope!
  My gude Lord Scroope, farewell!" he cried—
"I'll pay you for my lodging maill,
  When first we meet on the Border side."

Then shoulder high, with shout and cry,
  We bore him down the ladder lang;
At every stride Red Rowan made,
  I wot the Kinmont's airns play'd clang.

"O mony a time," quo' Kinmont Willie,
"I have ridden horse baith wild and wood;
But a rougher beast than Red Rowan
I ween my legs have ne'er bestrode.

"And mony a time," quo' Kinmont Willie,
"I've prick'd a horse out oure the furs;
But since the day I back'd a steed,
I never wore sic cumbrous spurs."

We scarce had won the Staneshaw-bank,
When a' the Carlisle bells were rung,
And a thousand men on horse and foot
Cam wi' the keen Lord Scroope along.

Buccleuch has turn'd to Eden Water,
Even where it flow'd frae bank to brim,
And he has plunged in wi' a' his band,
And safely swam them through the stream.

He turn'd him on the other side,
And at Lord Scroope his glove flung he—
"If ye like na my visit in merry England,
In fair Scotland come visit me!"

All sore astonish'd stood Lord Scroope,
He stood as still as rock of stane;
He scarcely dared to trew his eyes,
When through the water they had gane.

"He is either himsell a devil frae hell,
 Or else his mother a witch maun be;
I wadna have ridden that wan water
 For a' the gowd in Christentie."

DICK O' THE COW.

From Caw's *Poetical Museum*, p. 22.

THE personage from whom this ballad is named was jester to Lord Scroop, who was warden of the West Marches of England from 1590 to 1603. The Laird's Jock, that is John, the son of the Laird of Mangerton, "appears as one of the *men of name* in Liddesdale, in the list of the Border Clans, 1597."

Dick o' the Cow is closely connected with *Jock o' the Side* and *Hobie Noble*, which follow shortly after. All three were first printed in Caw's *Museum*, and seem to have been contributed by a Mr. Elliot, a Liddesdale gentleman, to whom Sir W. Scott acknowledges many obligations. We are told that both *Dick o' the Cow* and *Jock o' the Side* were until lately so popular in Liddesdale with all classes of people, that they were invariably sung, from beginning to end, at every festive meeting.

The ballad of *Dick o' the Cow* was well known in England as early as 1596.

"An allusion to it likewise occurs in PARROT'S *Laquei Ridiculosi*, or *Springes for Woodcocks;* London, 1613.

> "Owenus wondreth since he came to Wales,
> What the description of this isle should be,
> That nere had seen but mountains, hills, and dales,
> Yet would he boast, and stand on pedigree,
> From Rice ap Richard, sprung from *Dick a Cow*,
> Be cod, was right gud gentleman, look ye now!"
> *Epigr.* 76.—SCOTT.

Now Liddisdale has lyan lang in,
There is nae riding there at a';
The horses are grown sae lidder fat,
They downa stur out o' the sta'.

Then Johnie Armstrong to Willie can say—
"Billie, a riding then we'll gae;
England and us has been lang at a feid;
Ablins we'll hit on some bootie."

Then they're com'd on to Hutton Ha',
They rade the proper place about;
But the laird he was the wiser man,
For he had left nae gear without.

Then he had left nae gear to steal,
Except sax sheep upon a lee:
Quo' Johnie—"I'd rather in England die,
Ere thir sax sheep gae t' Liddisdale wi' me.

"But how ca'd they the man we last met,
Billie, as we cam o'er the know?"
"That same he is an innocent fool,
And some men ca' him Dick o' the Cow."

"That fool has three as good ky o' his ain,
As there's in a' Cumberland, billie," quo' he:
"Betide me life, betide me death,
These three ky shall gae t' Liddisdale wi' me."

Then they're com'd on to the poor fool's house,
And they hae broken his wa's sae wide;
They have loos'd out Dick o' the Cow's three ky,
And tane three co'erlets aff his wife's bed.

Then on the morn, whan the day was light,
The shouts and cries rose loud and hie:
"O had thy tongue, my wife," he says,
"And o' thy crying let me be!

"O had thy tongue, my wife," he says,
"And of thy crying let me be;
And aye that where thou wants a cow,
In good sooth I'll bring thee three."

Then Dickie's com'd on for's lord and master,
And I wat a dreirie fool was he;
"Now had thy tongue, my fool," he says,
"For I may not stand to jest wi' thee."

"Shame speed a' your jesting, my lord!" quo' Dickie,
"For nae sic jesting grees wi' me;
Liddisdale's been i' my house last night,
And they hae tane my three ky frae me.

"But I may nae langer in Cumberland dwell,
To be your poor fool and your leal,
Unless ye gi' me leave, my lord,
T' gae t' Liddisdale and steal."

"I gi' thee leave, my fool," he says;
"Thou speakest against my honour and me,
Unless thou gi' me thy trowth and thy hand,
Thou'lt steal frae nane but wha sta' frae thee."

"There is my trowth, and my right hand!
My head shall hang on Hairibee,
I'll near cross Carlisle sands again,
If I steal frae a man but wha sta' frae me."

Dickie's tane leave at lord and master,
And I wat a merry fool was he;
He's bought a bridle and a pair o' new spurs,
And pack'd them up in his breek thigh.

Then Dickie's come on for Pudding-burn,
E'en as fast as he might drie;

54. The place of execution at Carlisle.—P. M.
61. This was a house of strength held by the Armstrongs.

Now Dickie's come on for Pudding-burn,
Where there were thirty Armstrongs and three.

"O what's this com'd o' me now?" quo' Dickie;
"What meikle wae's this happen'd o' me? quo' he;
Where here is but ae innocent fool,
And there is thirty Armstrongs and three!"

Yet he's com'd up to the ha' amang them a',
Sae weil he's became his curtesie!
"Weil may ye be, my good Laird's Jock!
But the de'il bless a' your companie.

"I'm come to 'plain o' your man, fair Johnie Armstrong,
And syne o' his billie Willie," quo' he;
"How they hae been i' my house the last night,
And they hae tane my three ky frae me."

Quo' Johnie Armstrong, "We will him hang;"
"Na then," quo' Willie, "we'll him slae;"
But up and bespake anither young man,
"We'll gie 'im his batts, and let him gae."

Then up and bespake the good Laird's Jock,
The best falla in a' the companie;

The ruins at present form a sheep-fold on the farm of Reidsmoss, belonging to the Duke of Buccleuch.—S.

"Sit thy ways down a little while, Dickie,
  And a piece o' thy ain cow's hough I'll gi' thee."

But Dickie's heart it grew sae great,
  That ne'er a bit o't he dought to eat;
Then Dickie was ware o' an auld peat-house,
  Where a' the night he thought for to sleep.

Then Dickie was ware o' an auld peat-house,
  Where a' the night he thought for to ly;
And a' the prayers the poor fool pray'd,
  "I wish I had amense for my ain three ky!"

Then it was the use of Pudding-burn,
  And the house of Mangerton, all haill,
These that cam na at the first ca',
  They got nae mair meat t' the neist meal.

The lads, that hungry and weary were,
  Aboon the door-head they hang the key;
Dickie he took good notice to that,
  Says—"There's a bootie yonder for me."

Then Dickie into the stable is gane,
  Where there stood thirty horses and three;
He has tied them a' wi' St. Mary's knot,
  A' these horses but barely three.

94. The Laird of Mangerton was chief of the clan Armstrong.—S.

103. Hamstringing a horse is termed, in the Border dialect,

He has tied them a' wi' St. Mary's knot,
A' these horses but barely three;
He's loupen on ane, tane anither in hand,
And out at the door and gane is Dickie.

Then on the morn, whan the day grew light,
The shouts and cries rose loud and hie—
"O where's that thief?" quo' the good Laird's Jock,
"Tell me the truth and the veritie!"

"O where's that thief?" quo' the good Laird's Jock;
"See unto me ye dinna lie!"—
"Dickie's been i' the stable last night,
And has my brother's horse and mine frae me."

"Ye wad ne'er be tall'd," quo' the good Laird's Jock;
"Have ye not found my tales fu' leel?
Ye wad ne'er out o' England bide,
Till crooked, and blind, and a' wad steal."

tying him with St. Mary's knot. Dickie used this cruel expedient to prevent a pursuit. It appears from the narration, that the horses left unhurt, belonged to fair Johnie Armstrang, his brother Willie, and the Laird's Jock—of which Dickie carried off two, and left that of the Laird's Jock, probably out of gratitude for the protection he had afforded him on his arrival.—S.

"But lend me thy bay," Johnie Armstrong can say;
"There's nae horse loose in the stable but he;
And I'll either bring Dick o' the Cow again,
Or the day is come that he shall die."

"To lend thee my bay!" the Laird's Jock can say,
"He's worth baith goud and good monie:
Dick o' the Cow has away twa horse:
I wish na thou may make him three."

He's tane the laird's jack on his back,
A twa-handed sword that hang by his thigh;
He's tane the steel cap on his head,
And on is he gane to follow Dickie.

Then Dickie was na a mile aff the town,
I wat a mile but barely three,
Till he's o'ertane by Johnie Armstrong,
Hand for hand, on Cannobie lee.

"Abide, abide now, Dickie, than,
The day is come that thou maun die;"
Then Dickie look'd o'er his left shoulder,
"Johnie, has thou any moe in companie?

"There is a preacher in our chapel,
And a' the lee-lang day teaches he:

136. A rising-ground on Cannobie, on the borders of Liddesdale.—P. M.

Whan day is gane and night is come,
  There's ne'er ae word I mark but three.

"The first and second is—Faith and Conscience;
  The third—Ne'er let a traitour free:
But, Johnie, what faith and conscience hadst thou,
  Whan thou took my three ky frae me?

"And when thou had tane away my three ky,
  Thou thought in thy heart thou was no well sped,
But sent thy billie Willie o'er the know,
  And he took three co'erlets aff my wife's bed."

Then Johnie let a spear fa' laigh by his thigh,
  Thought weil to hae slain the innocent, I trow;
But the powers above were mair than he,
  For he ran but the poor fool's jerkin through.

Together they ran, or ever they blan,
  This was Dickie the fool and he;
Dickie coud na win to him wi' the blade o' the sword,
  But feld 'im wi' the plumet under the eie.

Now Dickie has feld fair Johnie Armstrong,
  The prettiest man in the south countrie;
"Gramercy!" then can Dickie say,
  "I had but twa horse, thou has made me three."

He has tane the laird's jack aff his back,
  The twa-handed sword that hang by his thigh;
He has tane the steel cap aff his head—
  "Johnie, I'll tell my master I met wi' thee."

When Johnie wakened out o' his dream,
  I wat a drierie man was he:
"And is thou gane, now, Dickie, than?
  The shame gae in thy companie!

"And is thou gane, now, Dickie, than?
  The shame gae in thy companie!
For if I should live this hundred years,
  I ne'er shall fight wi' a fool after thee."

Then Dickie's come hame to lord and master,
  E'en as fast as he may drie;
"Now, Dickie, I'll neither eat nor drink,
  Till hie hanged thou shalt be."

"The shame speed the liars, my lord!" quo' Dickie;
  "That was no the promise ye made to me!
For I'd ne'er gane t' Liddisdale t' steal,
  Till I had got my leave at thee."

"But what gard thou steal the Laird's Jock's horse?
  And, limmer, what gard thou steal him?" quo' he;

"For lang might thou in Cumberland dwelt,
Ere the Laird's Jock had stawn frae thee."

"Indeed I wat ye lied, my lord!
And e'en sae loud as I hear ye lie!
I wan him frae his man, fair Johnie Armstrong,
Hand for hand, on Cannobie lee.

"There's the jack was on his back,
This twa-handed sword that hang laigh by his thigh,
And there's the steel cap was on his head;
I hae a' these takens to let thee see."

188. The commendation of the Laird's Jock's honesty seems but indifferently founded; for, in July, 1586, a bill was fouled against him, Dick of Dryup, and others, by the Deputy of Bewcastle, at a warden-meeting, for 400 head of cattle taken in open foray from the Drysike in Bewcastle: and in September, 1587, another complaint appears at the instance of one Andrew Rutlege of the Nook, against the Laird's Jock, and his accomplices, for 50 kine and oxen, besides furniture, to the amount of 100 merks sterling. See Bell's MSS., as quoted in the *History of Cumberland and Westmoreland.* In Sir Richard Maitland's poem against the thieves of Liddesdale, he thus commemorates the Laird's Jock:—

"They spuilye puir men of their pakis,
They leif them nocht on bed nor bakis:
Baith hen and cok,
With reil and rok,
The *Lairdis Jock*
All with him takis."—S.

"If that be true thou to me tells,
(I trow thou dare na tell a lie,)
I'll gi' thee twenty punds for the good horse,
Weil tel'd in thy cloak lap shall be.

"And I'll gi' thee ane o' my best milk-ky,
To maintain thy wife and children three;
And that may be as good, I think,
As ony twa o' thine might be."

"The shame speed the liers, my lord!" quo' Dickie;
"Trow ye aye to make a fool o' me?
I'll either hae thirty punds for the good horse,
Or he's gae t' Mortan fair wi' me."

He's gi'en him thirty punds for the good horse,
All in goud and good monie;
He has gi'en him ane o' his best milk-ky,
To maintain his wife and children three.

Then Dickie's came down through Carlisle town,
E'en as fast as he might drie:
The first o' men that he met with,
Was my Lord's brother, Bayliff Glozenburrie.

"Weil may ye be, my gude Ralph Scroope!"—
"Welcome, my brother's fool!" quo' he:

"Where did thou get fair Johnie Armstrong's horse?"
"Where did I get him, but steal him," quo' he.

"But wilt thou sell me fair Johnie Armstrong's horse?
And, billie, wilt thou sell him to me?" quo' he:
"Aye, and tell me the monie on my cloak lap:
For there's no ae fardin I'll trust thee."

"I'll gi' thee fifteen punds for the good horse,
Weil tel'd on thy cloak lap shall be;
And I'll gi' thee ane o' my best milk-ky,
To maintain thy wife and children three."

"The shame speed the liers, my lord!" quo' Dickie;
"Trow ye aye to make a fool o' me?" quo' he;
"I'll either hae thirty punds for the good horse,
Or he's gae t' Mortan fair wi' me."

He's gi'en him thirty punds for the gude horse,
All in goud and good monie;
He has gi'en him ane o' his best milk-ky,
To maintain his wife and children three.

Then Dickie lap a loup fu' hie,
And I wat a loud laugh laughed he—

"I wish the neck o' the third horse were broken,
For I hae a better o' my ain, if better can be."

Then Dickie's com'd hame to his wife again,
Judge ye how the poor fool sped;
He has gi'en her three score English punds,
For the three auld co'erlets was tane aff her bed.

"Hae, tak thee these twa as good ky,
I trow, as a' thy three might be;
And yet here is [a] white-footed nagie,
I think he'll carry baith thee and me.

"But I may nae langer in Cumberland bide;
The Armstrongs they'll hang me hie:"—
So Dickie's tane leave at lord and master,
And [at] Burgh under Stanmuir there dwells he.

JOCK O' THE SIDE.

From Caw's *Poetical Museum*, p. 145.

THE rescue of a prisoner from the hands of justice was a very favourite subject with ballad-makers, and, it is to be feared, no uncommon event in the actual experience of the police of former days. We have in the fifth volume seen how such an affair was conducted by Robin Hood and his associates; and in *Kinmont Willie* have had an authenticated account of a remarkable exploit of this description at the close of the reign of Elizabeth. The two ballads which follow have this same theme; but only the authority of tradition. *Jock o' the Side* has one circumstance in common with *Kinmont Willie*—the daring passage of the river: with *Archie of Ca'field* it agrees throughout.

Jock o' the Side would seem to have been nephew to the Laird of Mangertoun (the chief of the clan Armstrong), and consequently cousin to the Laird's Jock. Scott suggests that he was probably brother to Christie of the Syde, mentioned in the list of Border clans, 1597. Both of these worthies receive special notice in Maitland's complaint *Against the Thieves of Liddisdale.*

> "He is weil kend, Johne of the Syde;
> A greater thief did never ryde;
> He nevir tyris
> For to brek byris,
> Our muir and myris
> Ouir gude ane guide."

Scott has pointed out that Jock o' the Side assisted the Earl of Westmoreland in his escape after his insurrection with the Earl of Northumberland, in the twelfth year of Elizabeth.

"Now Liddisdale has ridden a raid,
But I wat they had better staid at hame;
For Mitchel o' Winfield he is dead,
And my son Johnie is prisoner ta'en."

For Mangerton-House Auld Downie is gane,
Her coats she has kilted up to her knee;
And down the water wi' speed she rins,
While tears in spaits fa' fast frae her eie.

Then up and bespake the Lord Mangerton,
"What news, what news, sister Downie, to me?"
"Bad news, bad news, my Lord Mangerton;
Mitchel is kill'd, and tane they hae my son Johnie."

"Ne'er fear, sister Downie," quo' Mangerton;
"I hae yokes of oxen, four and twentie;
My barns, my byres, and my faulds, a' weel fill'd,
And I'll part wi' them a', ere Johnie shall die.

"Three men I'll take to set him free,
Weel harness'd a' wi' best o' steel;
The English rogues may hear, and drie
The weight o' their braid-swords to feel.

"The Laird's Jock ane, the Laird's Wat twa,
O Hobie Noble, thou ane maun be;
Thy coat is blue, thou has been true,
Since England banish'd thee, to me."

Now Hobie was an English man,
In Bewcastle-dale was bred and born;

But his misdeeds they were sae great,
They banish'd him ne'er to return.

Lord Mangerton them orders gave,
"Your horses the wrang way maun a' be shod;
Like gentlemen ye must not seem,
But look like corn-caugers gawn ae road.

"Your armour gude ye maunna shaw,
Nor ance appear like men o' weir;
As country lads be all array'd,
Wi' branks and brecham on ilk mare."

Sae now a' their horses are shod the wrang way,
And Hobie has mounted his grey sae fine;
Jock his lively bay, Wat's on his white horse behind,
And on they rode for the water o' Tyne.

At the Cholerford they a' light down,
And there, wi' the help o' the light o' the moon,
A tree they cut, wi' fifteen naggs upo' ilk side,
To climb up the wa' o' Newcastle town.

But when they cam to Newcastle town,
And were alighted at the wa',
They fand their tree three ells o'er laigh,
They fand their stick baith short and sma'.

41. Cholerford is a ford on the Tyne, above Hexham.—S.

Then up and spake the Laird's ain Jock,
  "There's naething for't, the gates we maun force;"
But when they cam the gates unto,
  A proud porter withstood baith men and horse.

His neck in twa I wat they hae wrung,
  Wi' hand or foot he ne'er play'd paw;
His life and his keys at anes they hae tane,
  And cast his body ahind the wa'.

Now soon they reach Newcastle jail,
  And to the pris'ner thus they call;
"Sleips thou, wakes thou, Jock o' the Side,
  Or is thou wearied o' thy thrall?"

Jock answers thus, wi' dolefu' tone—
  "Aft, aft I wake—I seldom sleip:
But wha's this kens my name sae weel,
  And thus to hear my waes do[es] seek?"

Then up and spake the good Laird's Jock,
  "Ne'er fear ye now, my billie," quo' he;
"For here's the Laird's Jock, the Laird's Wat,
  And Hobie Noble, come to set thee free."

"O had thy tongue, and speak nae mair,
  And o' thy tawk now let me be;
For if a' Liddisdale were here the night,
  The morn's the day that I maun die.

"Full fifteen stane o' Spanish iron,
They hae laid a' right sair on me;
Wi' locks and keys I am fast bound
Into this dungeon mirk and drearie."

"Fear ye no that," quo' the Laird's Jock;
"A faint heart ne'er wan a fair ladie;
Work thou within, we'll work without,
And I'll be bound we set thee free."

The first strong dore that they came at,
They loosed it without a key;
The next chain'd dore that they cam at,
They gar'd it a' in flinders flee.

The pris'ner now, upo' his back,
The Laird's Jock's gotten up fu' hie;
And down the stair, him, irons and a',
Wi' nae sma' speed and joy brings he.

Now, Jock, I wat," quo' Hobie Noble,
"Part o' the weight ye may lay on me;"
"I wat weel no!" quo' the Laird's Jock,
"I count him lighter than a flee."

Sae out at the gates they a' are gane,
The pris'ner's set on horseback hie;
And now wi' speed they've tane the gate,
While ilk ane jokes fu' wantonlie.

"O Jock, sae winsomely's ye ride,
Wi' baith your feet upo' ae side!
Sae weel's ye're harness'd, and sae trig,
In troth ye sit like ony bride!"

The night, tho' wat, they didna mind,
But hied them on fu' mirrilie,
Until they cam to Cholerford brae,
Where the water ran like mountains hie.

But when they came to Cholerford,
There they met with an auld man;
Says—"Honest man, will the water ride?
Tell us in haste, if that ye can."

"I wat weel no," quo' the good auld man;
"Here I hae liv'd this threty yeirs and three,
And I ne'er yet saw the Tyne sae big,
Nor rinning ance sae like a sea."

Then up and spake the Laird's saft Wat,
The greatest coward in the company—
"Now halt, now halt, we needna try't;
The day is com'd we a' maun die!"

"Poor faint-hearted thief!" quo' the Laird's ain Jock,
"There'll nae man die but he that's fie;
I'll lead ye a' right safely through;
Lift ye the pris'ner on ahint me."

Sae now the water they a' hae tane,
By anes and twas they a' swam through ;
" Here are we a' safe," says the Laird's Jock,
"And, poor faint Wat, what think ye now ? "

They scarce the ither side had won,
When twenty men they saw pursue ;
Frae Newcastle town they had been sent,
A' English lads, right good and true.

But when the land-sergeant the water saw,
" It winna ride, my lads," quo' he ;
Then out he cries—" Ye the pris'ner may take,
But leave the irons, I pray, to me."

" I wat weel no," cry'd the Laird's Jock,
" I'll keep them a' ; shoon to my mare they'll be :
My good grey mare—for I am sure,
She's bought them a' fu' dear frae thee."

Sae now they're away for Liddisdale,
E'en as fast as they cou'd them hie ;
The pris'ner 's brought to his ain fire-side,
And there o's airns they make him free.

169. The land-sergeant (mentioned also in *Hobbie Noble*) was an officer under the warden, to whom was committed the apprehending of delinquents, and the care of the public peace.—S.

"Now, Jock, my billie," quo' a' the three,
"The day was com'd thou was to die;
But thou's as weel at thy ain fire-side,
Now sitting, I think, 'tween thee and me."

They hae gard fill up ae punch-bowl,
And after it they maun hae anither,
And thus the night they a' hae spent,
Just as they had been brither and brither.

ARCHIE OF CA'FIELD.

Minstrelsy of the Scottish Border, ii. 116.

This is substantially the same story as *Jock o' the Side.* Another version from Motherwell's collection is subjoined.

"Ca'field, or Calfield," says Scott, "is a place in Wauchopdale, belonging of old to the Armstrongs. In the account betwixt the English and Scottish Marches, Jock and Geordie of Ca'field, then called Calf-hill, are repeatedly marked as delinquents. *History of Westmoreland and Cumberland*, vol. i. Introduction, p. 33."

As I was a-walking mine alane,
It was by the dawning of the day,
I heard twa brithers make their mane,
And I listen'd weel to what they did say.

The youngest to the eldest said,
  "Blythe and merrie how can we be?
There were three brithren of us born,
  And ane of us is condemn'd to die."

"And ye wad be merrie, and ye wad be sad,
  What the better wad billy Archie be?
Unless I had thirty men to mysell,
  And a' to ride in my cumpanie.

"Ten to hald the horses' heads,
  And other ten the watch to be,
And ten to break up the strong prison,
  Where billy Archie he does lie."

Then up and spak him mettled John Hall,
  (The luve of Teviotdale aye was he,)
"An I had eleven men to mysell,
  It's aye the twalt man I wad be."

Then up bespak him coarse Ca'field,
  (I wot and little gude worth was he,)
"Thirty men is few anew,
  And a' to ride in our companie."

There was horsing, horsing in haste,
  And there was marching on the lee,

17. Mettled John Hall, from the laigh Teviotdale, is perhaps John Hall of Newbigging, mentioned in the list of Border clans as one of the chief men of name residing on the Middle Marches in 1597.—S.

Until they cam to Murraywhate,
And they lighted there right speedilie.

"A smith! a smith!" Dickie he cries,
"A smith, a smith, right speedilie,
To turn back the caukers of our horses' shoon;
For it's unkensome we wad be."

"There lives a smith on the water-side,
Will shoe my little black mare for me;
And I've a crown in my pocket,
And every groat of it I wad gie."

"The night is mirk, and it's very mirk,
And by candle-light I canna weel see;
The night is mirk, and it's very pit mirk,
And there will never a nail ca' right for me."

"Shame fa' you and your trade baith,
Canna beet a good fellow by your mystery;
But leeze me on thee, my little black mare,
Thou's worth thy weight in gold to me."

There was horsing, horsing in haste,
And there was marching upon the lee,
Until they cam to Dumfries port,
And they lighted there right speedilie.

"There's five of us will hold the horse,
And other five will watchmen be:"

"But wha's the man among ye a',
Will gae to the Tolbooth door wi' me?"

O up then spak him mettled John Hall,
(Frae the Laigh Teviotdale was he,)
"If it should cost my life this very night,
I'll gae to the Tolbooth door wi' thee."

"Be of gude cheir, now, Archie, lad,
Be of gude cheir, now, dear billie!
Work thou within, and we without,
And the morn thou'se dine at Ca'field wi' me."

O Jockie Hall stepp'd to the door,
And he bended low back his knee,
And he made the bolts, the door hang on,
Loup frae the wa' right wantonlie.

He took the prisoner on his back,
And down the Tolbooth stair cam he:
The black mare stood ready at the door,
I wot a foot ne'er stirred she.

They laid the links out owre her neck,
And that was her gold twist to be;
And they cam doun thro' Dumfries toun,
And wow but they cam speedilie!

70. The *gold twist* means the small gilded chains drawn ross the chest of a war-horse, as a part of his caparison.—S.

The live-lang night these twelve men rade,
  And aye till they were right wearie,
Until they cam to the Murraywhate,
  And they lighted there right speedilie.

"A smith! a smith!" then Dickie he cries,
  "A smith, a smith, right speedilie,
To file the irons frae my dear brither,
  For forward, forward we wad be."

They hadna filed a shackle of iron,
  A shackle of iron but barely thrie,
When out and spak young Simon brave,
  "O dinna you see what I do see?

"Lo! yonder comes Lieutenant Gordon,
  Wi' a hundred men in his companie;
This night will be our lyke-wake night,
  The morn the day we a' maun die."

O there was mounting, mounting in haste,
  And there was marching upon the lee;
Until they cam to Annan water,
  And it was flowing like the sea.

"My mare is young and very skeigh,
  And in o' the weil she will drown me;
But ye'll take mine, and I'll take thine,
  And sune through the water we sall be."

Then up and spak him, coarse Ca'field,
(I wot and little gude worth was he,)
"We had better lose ane than lose a' the lave;
We'll lose the prisoner, we'll gae free."

"Shame fa' you and your lands baith!
Wad ye e'en your lands to your born billy?
But hey! bear up, my bonnie black mare,
And yet thro' the water we sall be."

Now they did swim that wan water,
And wow but they swam bonnilie!
Until they cam to the other side,
And they wrang their cloathes right drunkily.

"Come thro', come thro,' Lieutenant Gordon!
Come thro' and drink some wine wi' me!
For there is an ale-house here hard by,
And it shall not cost thee ae penny."

"Throw me my irons," quo' Lieutenant Gordon;
"I wot they cost me dear eneugh;"
"The shame a ma," quo' mettled John Ha',
"They'll be gude shackles to my pleugh."

"Come thro', come thro', Lieutenant Gordon!
Come thro', and drink some wine wi' me!
Yestreen I was your prisoner,
But now this morning am I free."

BILLIE ARCHIE.

Motherwell's *Minstrelsy*, p. 335.

A North-Country version of the preceding ballad. There is another copy in Buchan's larger collec tion, i. 111, *The Three Brothers.*

"Seven years have I loved my love,
And seven years my love's loved me,
But now to-morrow is the day
That Billie Archie, my love, must die."

Out then spoke him Little Dickie,
And still the best fellow was he;
"Had I but five men and mysell,
Then we would borrow Billie Archie."

Out it spoke him Caff o' Lin,
And still the worst fellow was he;
"Ye shall have five men and yoursell,
And I will bear you companie.

"We will not go like to dragoons,
Nor yet will we like grenadiers;
But we will go like corn-dealers,
And lay our brechams on our meares.

"And twa of us will watch the road,
  And other twa between will gang,
And I will go to jail-house door,
  And hold the prisoner unthought lang."

"Wha is this at the jail-house door,
  Sa weel as they do ken the gin?"
"It's I mysell," said him Little Dickie,
  "And O sae fain 's I would be in!"

"Awa, awa, now, Little Dickie,
  Awa, let all your folly be;
If the Lord Lieutenant come on you,
  Like unto dogs he'll cause you die."

"Hold you, hold you, Billy Archie,
  And now let all your folly be;
Though I die without, you'll not die within,
  For borrowed shall your body be."

"Awa, awa, now, Little Dickie,
  Awa, let all this folly be;
An hundred pounds of Spanish irons
  Is all bound on my fair bodie."

Wi' plough coulters and gavelocks
  They made the jail-house door to flee;
"And in God's name," said Little Dickie,
  "Cast you the prisoner behind me."

They had not rade a great way off,
  With all the haste that ever could be,
Till they espied the Lord Lieutenant,
  With a hundred men in companie.

But when they cam to wan water,
  It now was rumbling like the sea;
Then were they got into a strait,
  As great a strait as well could be.

Then out did speak him Caff o' Lin,
  And aye the warst fellow was he:
"Now God be with my wife and bairns,
  For fatherless my babes will be.

"My horse is young, he cannot swim;
  The water's deep, and will not wade;
My children must be fatherless,
  My wife a widow, whate'er betide."

O then cried out him Little Dickie,
  And still the best fellow was he:
"Take you my mare, I'll take your horse,
  And Devil drown my mare and thee!"

Now they have taken the wan water,
  Though it was roaring like the sea;
And when they gat to the other side,
  I wat they bragged right crousilie.

"Come thro', come thro', now, Lord Lieutenant,
O do come thro', I pray of thee;
There is an alehouse not far off,
We'll dine you and your companie."

"Awa, awa, now, Little Dickie,
O now let all your taunting be;
There's not a man in the king's army
That would have tried what's done by thee.

"Cast back, cast back my fetters again,
Cast back my fetters, I say to thee;
And get you gane the way you came,
I wish no prisoners like to thee."

"I have a mare, she's called Meg,
The best in all our low countrie;
If she gang barefoot till they're done,
An ill death may your Lordship die."

HOBIE NOBLE.

From Caw's *Poetical Museum*, p. 193.

"We have seen the hero of this ballad act a distinguished part in the deliverance of Jock o' the Side, and are now to learn the ungrateful return which the Armstrongs made him for his faithful services. Halbert, or Hobbie, Noble appears to have been one of those numerous English outlaws, who, being forced to fly their own country, had established themselves on the Scottish Borders. As Hobbie continued his depredations upon the English, they bribed some of his hosts, the Armstrongs, to decoy him into England under pretence of a predatory expedition. He was there delivered, by his treacherous companions, into the hands of the officers of justice, by whom he was conducted to Carlisle, and executed next morning. The Laird of Mangertoun, with whom Hobbie was in high favour, is said to have taken a severe revenge upon the traitors who betrayed him. The principal contriver of the scheme, called here Sim o' the Maynes, fled into England from the resentment of his chief; but experienced there the common fate of a traitor, being himself executed at Carlisle, about two months after Hobbie's death. Such is, at least, the tradition of Liddesdale. Sim o' the Maynes appears among the Armstrongs of Whitauch, in Liddesdale, in the list of Clans so often alluded to."—*Minstrelsy of the Scottish Border*, ii. 90.

Foul fa' the breast first treason bred in!
  That Liddisdale may safely say;
For in it there was baith meat and drink,
  And corn unto our geldings gay.

We were stout-hearted men and true,
  As England it did often say;
But now we may turn our backs and fly,
  Since brave Noble is seld away.

Now Hobie he was an English man,
And born into Bewcastle dale;
But his misdeeds they were sae great,
They banish'd him to Liddisdale.

At Kershope foot the tryst was set,
Kershope of the lily lee;
And there was traitour Sim o' the Mains,
With him a private companie.

Then Hobie has graith'd his body weel,
I wat it was wi' baith good iron and steel;
And he has pull'd out his fringed grey,
And there, brave Noble, he rade him weel.

Then Hobie is down the water gane,
E'en as fast as he may drie;
Tho' they shoud a' brusten and broken their hearts,
Frae that tryst Noble he would not be.

"Weel may ye be, my feiries five!
And aye, what is your wills wi' me?"
Then they cry'd a' wi' ae consent,
"Thou'rt welcome here, brave Noble, to me.

13. Kershope-burn, where Hobbie met his treacherous companions, falls into the Liddel, from the English side, at a place called Turnersholm, where, according to tradition, tourneys and games of chivalry were often solemnized.—S.

15. The Mains was anciently a Border-keep, near Castletown, on the north side of the Liddel, but is now totally demolished.—S.

"Wilt thou with us in England ride,
And thy safe warrand we will be?
If we get a horse worth a hundred punds,
Upon his back that thou shalt be."

"I dare not with you into England ride,
The Land-sergeant has me at feid;
I know not what evil may betide,
For Peter of Whitfield, his brother, is dead.

"And Anton Shiel, he loves not me,
For I gat twa drifts of his sheep;
The great Earl of Whitfield loves me not,
For nae gear frae me he e'er could keep.

"But will ye stay till the day gae down,
Until the night come o'er the grund,
And I'll be a guide worth ony twa
That may in Liddisdale be fund.

"Tho' dark the night as pick and tar,
I'll guide ye o'er yon hills fu' hie,

38. For twa drifts of his sheep I gat.—P. M.

39. Whitfield is explained by Mr. Ellis of Otterbourne to be a large and rather wild manorial district in the extreme southwest part of Northumberland; the proprietor of which might be naturally called the Lord, though not *Earl* of Whitfield. I suspect, however, that the reciters may have corrupted the *great* Ralph Whitfield into Earl of Whitfield. Sir Matthew Whitfield of Whitfield, was Sheriff of Northumberland in 1433, and the estate continued in the family from the reign of Richard II. till about fifty years since.—S.

And bring ye a' in safety back,
  If you'll be true and follow me."

He's guided them o'er moss and muir,
  O'er hill and houp, and mony a down;
Til they came to the Foulbogshiel,
  And there, brave Noble, he lighted down.

Then word is gane to the Land-sergeant,
  In Askirton where that he lay—
"The deer that ye hae hunted lang
  Is seen into the Waste this day."

"Then Hobie Noble is that deer!
  I wat he carries the style fu' hie;
Aft has he beat your slough-hounds back,
  And set yourselves at little lee.

"Gar warn the bows of Hartlie-burn,
  See they shaft their arrows on the wa'!
Warn Willeva, and Spear Edom,
  And see the morn they meet me a'.

54. Askerton is an old castle, now ruinous, situated in the wilds of Cumberland, about seventeen miles north-east of Carlisle, amidst that mountainous and desolate tract of country bordering upon Liddesdale, emphatically termed the Waste of Bewcastle.—S.

63-67. Willeva and Speir Edom are small districts in Bewcastledale, through which also the Hartlie-burn takes its course. Conscouthart-Green, and Rodric-haugh, and the Foulbogshiel, are the names of places in the same wilds,

"Gar meet me on the Rodrie-haugh,
And see it be by break o' day;
And we will on to Conscowthart-Green,
For there, I think, we'll get our prey."

Then Hobie Noble has dream'd a dream,
In the Foulbogsheil where that he lay;
He thought his horse was 'neath him shot,
And he himself got hard away.

The cocks could crow, and the day could dawn,
And I wat so even down fell the rain;
If Hobie had no waken'd at that time,
In the Foulbogshiel he had been tane or slain.

"Get up, get up, my feiries five!
For I wat here makes a fu' ill day;
And the warst cloak of this companie,
I hope shall cross the Waste this day."

Now Hobie thought the gates were clear;
But, ever alas! it was not sae:
They were beset wi' cruel men and keen,
That away brave Noble could not gae.

"Yet follow me, my feiries five,
And see of me ye keep good ray;

through which the Scottish plunderers generally made their raids upon England.—S.

79, 87. clock.

And the worst cloak of this companie
  I hope shall cross the Waste this day."

There was heaps of men now Hobie before,
  And other heaps was him behind,
That had he been as wight as Wallace was,
  Away brave Noble he could not win.

Then Hobie he had but a laddies sword,
  But he did more than a laddies deed;
In the midst of Conscouthart-Green,
  He brake it o'er Jersawigham's head.

Now they have tane brave Hobie Noble,
  Wi' his ain bowstring they band him sae;
And I wat heart was ne'er sae sair,
  As when his ain five band him on the brae.

They have tane him for West Carlisle;
  They ask'd him if he knew the way;
Whate'er he thought, yet little he said;
  He knew the way as well as they.

They hae tane him up the Ricker-gate;
  The wives they cast their windows wide,
And ilka wife to anither can say,
  "That's the man loos'd Jock o' the Side!"

"Fy on ye, women! why ca' ye me man?
  For it's nae man that I'm used like;

105. A street in Carlisle.

I'm but like a forfoughen hound,
Has been fighting in a dirty syke."

Then they hae tane him up thro' Carlisle town,
And set him by the chimney fire;
They gave brave Noble a wheat loaf to eat,
And that was little his desire.

Then they gave him a wheat loaf to eat
And after that a can o' beer;
Then they cried a', wi' ae consent,
"Eat, brave Noble, and make good cheer.

"Confess my lord's horse, Hobie," they say,
"And the morn in Carlisle thou's no die;"
"How shall I confess them?" Hobie says,
"For I never saw them with mine eye."

Then Hobie has sworn a fu' great aith—
By the day that he was gotten or born,
He never had onything o' my lord's,
That either eat him grass or corn.

"Now fare thee weel, sweet Mangerton!
For I think again I'll ne'er thee see:
I wad betray nae lad alive,
For a' the goud in Christentie.

129. Of the Castle of Mangertoun, so often mentioned in these ballads, there are very few vestiges. It was situated on the banks of the Liddell, below Castletoun.—S.

"And fare thee weel, now Liddisdale,
Baith the hie land and the law!
Keep ye weel frae traitor Mains!
For goud and gear he'll sell ye a'.

"I'd rather be ca'd Hobie Noble,
In Carlisle, where he suffers for his faut,
Before I were ca'd traitor Mains,
That eats and drinks of meal and maut."

JAMIE TELFER

OF THE FAIR DODHEAD.

From *Minstrelsy of the Scottish Border*, ii. 3.

"There is another ballad, under the same title as the following, in which nearly the same incidents are narrated, with little difference, except that the honour of rescuing the cattle is attributed to the Liddesdale Elliots, headed by a chief, there called Martin Elliot of the Preakin Tower, whose son, Simon, is said to have fallen in the action. It is very possible, that both the Teviotdale Scotts, and the Elliots, were engaged in the affair, and that each claimed the honour of the victory.

"The Editor presumes, that the Willie Scott, here

mentioned, must have been a natural son of the Laird of Buccleuch."—S.

It fell about the Martinmas tyde,
  When our Border steeds get corn and hay,
The Captain of Bewcastle hath bound him to
    ryde,
  And he's ower to Tividale to drive a prey.

The first ae guide that they met wi',
  It was high up in Hardhaughswire;
The second guide that they met wi',
  It was laigh down in Borthwick water.

"What tidings, what tidings, my trusty guide?"
  "Nae tidings, nae tidings, I hae to thee;
But gin ye'll gae to the fair Dodhead,
  Mony a cow's cauf I'll let thee see."

And when they cam to the fair Dodhead,
  Right hastily they clam the peel;
They loosed the kye out, ane and a',
  And ranshackled the house right weel.

Now Jamie Telfer's heart was sair,
  The tear aye rowing in his ee;

6-8. Hardhaughswire is the pass from Liddesdale to the head of Teviotdale. Borthwick water is a stream which falls into the Tevoit three miles above Hawick.—S.

11. The Dodhead, in Selkirkshire, near Singlee, where there are still the vestiges of an old tower.—S.

He pled wi' the Captain to hae his gear,
  Or else revenged he wad be.

The Captain turned him round and leugh;
  Said—"Man, there's naething in thy house,
But ae auld sword without a sheath,
  That hardly now would fell a mouse."

The sun wasna up, but the moon was down,
  It was the gryming of a new-fa'n snaw,
Jamie Telfer has run ten myles a-foot,
  Between the Dodhead and the Stobs's Ha'.

And when he cam to the fair tower yate,
  He shouted loud, and cried weel hie,
Till out bespak auld Gibby Elliot—
  "Whae's this that brings the fraye to me?"

"It's I, Jamie Telfer, o' the fair Dodhead,
  And a harried man I think I be;
There's naething left at the fair Dodhead,
  But a waefu' wife and bairnies three."

"Gae seek your succour at Branksome Ha',
  For succour ye'se get nane frae me;

28. Stobs Hall, upon Slitterick, the seat of Sir William, of that clan. Jamie Telfer made his first application here, because he *seems* to have paid the proprietor of the castle *black-mail*, or protection money.—S.

37. The ancient family-seat of the Lairds of Buccleuch, near Hawick.—S.

Gae seek your succour where ye paid black-mail,
For, man, ye ne'er paid money to me."

Jamie has turned him round about,
I wat the tear blinded his ee—
"I'll ne'er pay mail to Elliot again,
And the fair Dodhead I'll never see!

"My hounds may a' rin masterless,
My hawks may fly frae tree to tree,
My lord may grip my vassal lands,
For there again maun I never be!"

He has turn'd him to the Tiviot side,
E'en as fast as he could drie,
Till he cam to the Coultart Cleugh,
And there he shouted baith loud and hie.

Then up bespak him auld Jock Grieve—
"Whae's this that brings the fraye to me?"
"It's I, Jamie Telfer o' the fair Dodhead,
A harried man I trow I be.

"There's naething left in the fair Dodhead,
But a greeting wife and bairnies three,
And sax poor ca's stand in the sta',
A' routing loud for their minnie."

45–48. See *Young Beichan*, vol. iv. p. 3.

51. The Coultart Cleugh is nearly opposite to Carlinrig, on the road between Hawick and Mosspaul.—S.

"Alack a wae!" quo' auld Jock Grieve,
  "Alack, my heart is sair for thee!
For I was married on the elder sister,
  And you on the youngest of a' the three."

Then he has ta'en out a bonny black,
  Was right weel fed with corn and hay,
And he's set Jamie Telfer on his back,
  To the Catslockhill to tak the fraye.

And whan he cam to the Catslockhill,
  He shouted loud, and cried weel hie,
Till out and spak him William's Wat—
  "O whae's this brings the fraye to me?"

"It's I, Jamie Telfer of the fair Dodhead,
  A harried man I think I be;
The Captain of Bewcastle has driven my gear;
  For God's sake rise, and succour me!"

"Alas for wae!" quoth William's Wat,
  "Alack, for thee my heart is sair!
I never cam by the fair Dodhead,
  That ever I fand thy basket bare."

He's set his twa sons on coal-black steeds,
  Himsell upon a freckled gray,
And they are on wi' Jamie Telfer,
  To Branksome Ha' to tak the fraye.

And when they cam to Branksome Ha',
They shouted a' baith loud and hie,
Till up and spak him auld Buccleuch,
Said—" Whae's this brings the fraye to me?"

" It's I, Jamie Telfer o' the fair Dodhead,
And a harried man I think I be;
There's nought left in the fair Dodhead,
But a greeting wife and bairnies three."

" Alack for wae!" quoth the gude auld lord,
" And ever my heart is wae for thee!
But fye, gar cry on Willie, my son,
And see that he come to me speedilie.

" Gar warn the water, braid and wide,
Gar warn it sune and hastilie;
They that winna ride for Telfer's kye,
Let them never look in the face o' me!

" Warn Wat o' Harden, and his sons,
Wi' them will Borthwick Water ride;
Warn Gaudilands, and Allanhaugh,
And Gilmanscleugh, and Commonside.

97. The *water*, in the mountainous districts of Scotland, is often used to express the banks of the river, which are the only inhabitable parts of the country. *To raise the water*, therefore, was to alarm those who lived along its side.—S.

101. The estates, mentioned in this verse, belonged to families of the name of Scott, residing upon the waters of Borthwick and Teviot, near the castle of their chief.—S.

"Ride by the gate at Priesthaughswire,
And warn the Currors o' the Lee;
As ye cum down the Hermitage Slack,
Warn doughty Willie o' Gorrinberry."

The Scotts they rade, the Scotts they ran,
Sae starkly and sae steadilie,
And aye the ower-word o' the thrang
Was—"Rise for Branksome readilie!"

The gear was driven the Frostylee up,
Frae the Frostylee unto the plain,
Whan Willie has look'd his men before,
And saw the kye right fast drivand.

"Whae drives thir kye?" gan Willie say,
"To make an outspeckle o' me?"
"It's I, the Captain o' Bewcastle, Willie;
I winna layne my name for thee."

"O will ye let Telfer's kye gae back?
Or will ye do aught for regard o' me?
Or, by the faith of my body," quo' Willie Scott,
"I'se ware my dame's cauf skin on thee."

105. The pursuers seem to have taken the road through the hills of Liddesdale, in order to collect forces, and intercept the forayers at the passage of the Liddel, on their return to Bewcastle. The Ritterford and Kershope-ford, after-mentioned, are noted fords on the river Liddel.—S.

113. The Frostylee is a brook, which joins the Teviot, near Mosspaul.—S.

"I winna let the kye gae back,
  Neither for thy love, nor yet thy fear;
But I will drive Jamie Telfer's kye,
  In spite of every Scott that's here."

"Set on them, lads!" quo' Willie than;
  "Fye, lads, set on them cruellie!
For ere they win to the Ritterford,
  Mony a toom saddle there sall be!"

Then til't they gaed, wi' heart and hand,
  The blows fell thick as bickering hail;
And mony a horse ran masterless,
  And mony a comely cheek was pale.

But Willie was stricken ower the head,
  And thro' the knapscap the sword has gane;
And Harden grat for very rage,
  Whan Willie on the grund lay slane.

But he's ta'en aff his gude steel cap,
  And thrice he's waved it in the air;
The Dinlay snaw was ne'er mair white
  Nor the lyart locks of Harden's hair.

"Revenge! revenge!" auld Wat 'gan cry;
  "Fye, lads, lay on them cruellie!
We'll ne'er see Tiviotside again,
  Or Willie's death revenged sall be."

143. The Dinlay is a mountain in Liddesdale.—S.

O mony a horse ran masterless,
The splinter'd lances flew on hie;
But or they wan ta the Kershope ford,
The Scotts had gotten the victory.

John o' Brigham there was slane,
And John o' Barlow, as I heard say;
And thirty mae o' the Captain's men
Lay bleeding on the grund that day.

The Captain was run through the thick of the thigh,
And broken was his right leg bane;
If he had lived this hundred years,
He had never been loved by woman again.

"Hae back the kye!" the Captain said;
"Dear kye, I trow, to some they be;
For gin I suld live a hundred years,
There will ne'er fair lady smile on me."

Then word is gane to the Captain's bride,
Even in the bower where that she lay,
That her lord was prisoner in enemy's land,
Since into Tividale he had led the way.

153. Perhaps one of the ancient family of Brougham, in Cumberland. The Editor has used some freedom with the original in the subsequent verse. The account of the Captain's disaster is rather too *naïve* for literal publication.—S.

"I wad lourd have had a winding-sheet,
  And helped to put it ower his head,
Ere he had been disgraced by the Border Scot,
  Whan he ower Liddel his men did lead!"

There was a wild gallant amang us a',
  His name was Watty wi' the Wudspurs,
Cried—"On for his house in Stanegirthside,
  If ony man will ride with us!"

When they cam to the Stanegirthside,
  They dang wi' trees, and burst the door;
They loosed out a' the Captain's kye,
  And set them forth our lads before.

There was an auld wyfe ayont the fire,
  A wee bit o' the Captain's kin—
"Whae dar loose out the Captain's kye,
  Or answer to him and his men?"

"It's I, Watty Wudspurs, loose the kye,
  I winna layne my name frae thee;
And I will loose out the Captain's kye,
  In scorn of a' his men and he."

Whan they cam to the fair Dodhead,
  They were a wellcum sight to see;
For instead of his ain ten milk kye,
  Jamie Telfer has gotten thirty and three.

175. A house belonging to the Foresters, situated on the English side of the Liddel.—S.

And he has paid the rescue shot,
Baith wi' goud and white monie;
And at the burial o' Willie Scott,
I wat was mony a weeping ee.

THE FRAY OF SUPORT.

From *Minstrelsy of the Scottish Border*, ii. 124.

"Of all the Border ditties which have fallen into the Editor's hands, this is by far the most uncouth and savage. It is usually chanted in a sort of wild recitative, except the burden, which swells into a long and varied howl, not unlike to a view hollo'. The words, and the very great irregularity of the stanza (if it deserves the name) sufficiently point out its intention and origin. An English woman, residing in Suport, near the foot of the Kers-hope, having been plundered in the night by a band of the Scottish moss-troopers, is supposed to convoke her servants and friends for the pursuit, or *Hot Trod;* upbraiding them, at the

196. An article in the list of attempts upon England, fouled by the Commissioners at Berwick, in the year 1587, may relate to the subject of the foregoing ballad.

October, 1582.

Thomas Musgrave, deputy of Bewcastle, and the tenants, against	Walter Scott, Laird of Buckluth, and his complices; for	200 kine and oxen, 300 gait and sheep.

Introduction to the History of Westmoreland and Cumberland, p. 31.—S.

same time, in homely phrase, for their negligence and security. The *Hot Trod* was followed by the persons who had lost goods, with blood-hounds and horns, to raise the country to help. They also used to carry a burning wisp of straw at a spear head, and to raise a cry, similar to the Indian war-whoop. It appears, from articles made by the Wardens of the English Marches, September 12th, in 6th of Edward VI., that all, on this cry being raised, were obliged to follow the fray, or chase, under pain of death. With these explanations, the general purport of the ballad may be easily discovered, though particular passages have become inexplicable, probably through corruptions introduced by reciters. The present text is collected from four copies, which differed widely from each other."—S.

SLEEP'RY Sim of the Lamb-hill,
And snoring Jock of Suport-mill,
Ye are baith right het and fou';
But my wae wakens na you.
Last night I saw a sorry sight—
Nought left me o' four-and-twenty gude ousen and ky,
My weel-ridden gelding, and a white quey,
But a toom byre and a wide,
And the twelve nogs on ilka side.
Fy, lads! shout a' a' a' a' a',
My gear's a' gane.

Weel may ye ken,
Last night I was right scarce o' men:

But Toppet Hob o' the Mains had guesten'd in
my house by chance;
I set him to wear the fore-door wi' the speir,
while I kept the back-door wi' the lance;
But they hae run him thro' the thick o' the thie,
and broke his knee-pan,
And the mergh o' his shin-bane has run down
on his spur-leather whang:
He's lame while he lives, and where'er he may
gang.
Fy, lads! shout a' a' a' a' a',
My gear's a' gane.

But Peenye, my gude son, is out at the Hagbut-
head,
His een glittering for anger like a fiery gleed;
Crying—"Mak sure the nooks
Of Maky's-muir crooks;
For the wily Scot takes by nooks, hooks, and
crooks.
Gin we meet a' together in a head the morn,
We'll be merry men."
Fy, lads! shout a' a' a' a' a',
My gear's a' gane.

There's doughty Cuddy in the Heugh-head,
Thou was aye gude at a need;
With thy brock-skin bag at thy belt,

32. The badger-skin pouch was used for carrying ammunition.—S.

Aye ready to mak a puir man help.
Thou maun awa' out to the Cauf-craigs,
(Where anes ye lost your ain twa naigs,)
And there toom thy brock-skin bag.
Fy, lads! shout a' a' a' a' a',
My gear's a' ta'en.

Doughty Dan o' the Houlet Hirst,
Thou was aye gude at a birst;
Gude wi' a bow, and better wi' a speir,
The bauldest March-man that e'er follow'd gear:
Come thou here.
Fy, lads! shout a' a' a' a' a',
My gear's a' gane.

Rise, ye carle coopers, frae making o' kirns and tubs,
In the Nicol forest woods.
Your craft hasna left the value of an oak rod,
But if you had ony fear o' God,
Last night ye hadna slept sae sound,
And let my gear be a' ta'en.
Fy, lads! shout a' a' a' a' a',
My gear's a' ta'en.

Ah! lads, we'll fang them a' in a net,
For I hae a' the fords o' Liddel set;
The Dunkin and the Door-loup,

47. A wood in Cumberland, in which Suport is situated. —S.

The Willie-ford, and the Water-slack,
The Black-rack and the Trout-dub of Liddel.
There stands John Forster, wi' five men at his back,
Wi bufft coat and cap of steil.
Boo! ca' at them e'en, Jock;
That ford's sicker, I wat weil.
Fy, lads! shout a' a' a' a' a',
My gear's a' ta'en.

Hoo! hoo! gar raise the Reid Souter, and Ringan's Wat,
Wi' a broad elshin and a wicker;
I wat weil they'll mak a ford sicker.
Sae, whether they be Elliots or Armstrangs,
Or rough-riding Scots, or rude Johnstones,
Or whether they be frae the Tarras or Ewsdale,
They maun turn and fight, or try the deeps o' Liddel.
Fy, lads! shout a' a' a' a' a',
My gear's a' ta'en.

"Ah! but they will play ye anither jigg,
For they will out at the big rig,
And thro' at Fargy Grame's gap."

76. Fergus Grame of Sowport, as one of the chief men of that clan, became security to Lord Scroope for the good behaviour of his friends and dependents, 8th January, 1662.—*Introduction to History of Westmoreland and Cumberland*, p. 111.—S.

But I hae another wile for that:
For I hae little Will, and Stalwart Wat,
And lang Aicky, in the Souter Moor,
Wi' his sleuth-dog sits in his watch right sure.
Shou'd the dog gie a bark,
He'll be out in his sark,
And die or won.
    Fy, lads! shout a' a' a' a' a',
    My gear's a' ta'en.

Ha! boys!—I see a party appearing—wha's yon?
Methinks it's the Captain of Bewcastle, and Jephtha's John,
Coming down by the foul steps of Catlowdie's loan:
They'll make a' sicker, come which way they will.
    Ha, lads! shout a' a' a' a' a',
    My gear's a' ta'en.

Captain Musgrave, and a' his band,
Are coming down by the Siller-strand,

87–8. According to the late Glenriddel's notes on this ballad, the office of Captain Bewcastle was held by the chief of the Nixons. Catlowdie is a small village in Cumberland, near the junction of the Esk and Liddel.—S.

92. This was probably the famous Captain Jack Musgrave, who had charge of the watch along the Cryssop, or Kershope, as appears from the order of the watches appointed by Lord Wharton, when Deputy-Warden-General, in the 6th Edward VI.—S.

And the Muckle toun-bell o' Carlisle is rung:
My gear was a' weel won,
And before it's carried o'er the Border, mony a man's gae down.
Fy, lads! shout a' a' a' a' a',
My gear's a' gane.

ROOKHOPE RYDE.

"A Bishopric Border song, composed in 1569, taken down from the chanting of George Collingwood the elder, late of Boltsburn, in the neighbourhood of Ryhope, who was interred at Stanhope, the 16th December, 1785.

"Rookhope is the name of a valley about five miles in length; at the termination of which, Rookhope burn empties itself into the river Wear, and is in the north part of the parish of Stanhope, in Weardale. Rookhope-head is the top of the vale."—Ritson.

The date of the event, says Sir W. Scott, is pre cisely ascertained to be (not 1569 but) the 6th of December, 1572, when the Tynedale robbers were encouraged to make a foray into Weardale in consequence of the confusion occasioned by the rebellion of Westmoreland and Northumberland.

From Ritson's *Bishopric Garland* (p. 54), with one

or two slight verbal improvements from the *Minstrelsy of the Scottish Border*, ii. 101.

ROOKHOPE stands in a pleasant place,
If the false thieves wad let it be,
But away they steal our goods apace,
And ever an ill death may they dee!

And so is the men of Thirlwall and Willie-haver,
And all their companies thereabout,
That is minded to do mischief,
And at their stealing stands not out.

But yet we will not slander them all,
For there is of them good enow;
It is a sore consumed tree
That on it bears not one fresh bough.

Lord God! is not this a pitiful case,
That men dare not drive their goods to the fell,
But limmer thieves drives them away,
That fears neither heaven nor hell?

5. Thirlwall, or Thirlitwall, is said by Fordun, the Scottish historian, to be a name given to the Picts' or Roman wall, from its having been thirled, or perforated, in ancient times, by the Scots and Picts.

Willie-haver, or Willeva, is a small district or township in the parish of Lanercost, near Bewcastledale, in Cumberland, mentioned in the ballad of *Hobie Noble*.—RITSON.

Lord, send us peace into the realm,
That every man may live on his own!
I trust to God, if it be his will,
That Weardale men may never be overthrown.

For great troubles they've had in hand,
With borderers pricking hither and thither,
But the greatest fray that e'er they had,
Was with the men of Thirlwall and Williehaver.

They gather'd together so royally,
The stoutest men and the best in gear;
And he that rade not on a horse,
I wat he rade on a weel-fed mear.

So in the morning, before they came out,
So weel I wot they broke their fast;
In the [forenoon they came] unto a bye fell,
Where some of them did eat their last.

When they had eaten aye and done,
They say'd some captains here needs must be:
Then they choosed forth Harry Corbyl,
And 'Symon Fell,' and Martin Ridley.

31. This would be about eleven o'clock, the usual dinner-hour in that period.—Ritson.

Then o'er the moss, where as they came,
  With many a brank and whew,
One of them could to another say,
  "I think this day we are men enew.

"For Weardale-men is a journey ta'en;
  They are so far out o'er yon fell,
That some of them's with the two earls,
  And others fast in Bernard castell.

"There we shall get gear enough,
  For there is nane but women at hame;
The sorrowful fend that they can make,
  Is loudly cries as they were slain."

43. The two Earls were Thomas Percy, Earl of Northumberland, and Charles Nevil, Earl of Westmoreland, who, on the 15th of November, 1569, at the head of their tenantry and others, took arms for the purpose of liberating Mary, Queen of Scots, and restoring the old religion. They besieged Barnard castle, which was, for eleven days, stoutly defended by Sir George Bowes, who, afterward, being appointed the Queen's marshal, hanged the poor constables and peasantry by dozens in a day, to the amount of 800. The Earl of Northumberland, betrayed by the Scots, with whom he had taken refuge, was beheaded at York, on the 22d of August, 1572; and the Earl of Westmoreland, deprived of the ancient and noble patrimony of the Nevils, and reduced to beggary, escaped over sea, into Flanders, and died in misery and disgrace, being the last of his family.—RITSON. See *The Rising in the North* and *Northumberland betrayed by Douglas.*

48. This is still the phraseology of Westmoreland: a *poorly* man, a *softly* day, and the like.—RITSON.

Then in at Rookhope-head they came,
  And there they thought tul a had their prey,
But they were spy'd coming over the Dry-rig,
  Soon upon Saint Nicolas' day.

Then in at Rookhope-head they came,
  They ran the forest but a mile;
They gather'd together in four hours
  Six hundred sheep within a while.

And horses I trow they gat,
  But either ane or twa,
And they gat them all but ane
  That belang'd to great Rowley.

That Rowley was the first man that did them spy,
  With that he raised a mighty cry;
The cry it came down Rookhope burn,
  And spread through Weardale hasteyly.

Then word came to the bailiff's house
  At the East-gate, where he did dwell;

52. The 6th of December.

66. Now a straggling village so called; originally, it would seem, the gate-house, or ranger's lodge, at the east entrance of Stanhope-park. At some distance from this place is West-gate, so called for a similar reason.—Ritson.

The mention of the bailiff's house at the East-gate is (were such a proof wanting) strongly indicative of the authenticity of the ballad. The family of Emerson of East-gath, a fief,

He was walk'd out to the Smale-burns,
Which stands above the Hanging-well.

His wife was wae when she heard tell,
So weel she wist her husband wanted gear;
She gar'd saddle him his horse in haste,
And neither forgot sword, jack, nor spear.

The bailiff got wit before his gear came,
That such news was in the land,
He was sore troubled in his heart,
That on no earth that he could stand.

His brother was hurt three days before,
With limmer thieves that did him prick;
Nineteen bloody wounds lay him upon,
What ferly was't that he lay sick?

But yet the bailiff shrinked nought,
But fast after them he did hye,
And so did all his neighbours near,
That went to bear him company.

But when the bailiff was gathered,
And all his company,

if I may so call it, held under the bishop, long exercised the office of bailiff of Wolsingham, the chief town and borough of Weardale, and of Forster, &c., under successive prelates.—Surtees.

68. A place in the neighbourhood of East-gate, known at present, as well as the Dry-rig, or Smale-burns.—Ritson.

They were numbered to never a man
  But forty under fifty.

The thieves was numbered a hundred men,
  I wat they were not of the worst
That could be choosed out of Thirlwall and Willie-
    haver,
  [I trow they were the very first.]

But all that was in Rookhope-head,
  And all that was i' Nuketon-cleugh,
Where Weardale-men o'ertook the thieves,
  And there they gave them fighting eneugh.

So sore they made them fain to flee,
  As many was 'a'' out of hand,
And, for tul have been at home again,
  They would have been in iron bands.

And for the space of long seven years
  As sore they mighten a' had their lives,
But there was never one of them
  That ever thought to have seen their 'wives.'

About the time the fray began,
  I trow it lasted but an hour,
Till many a man lay weaponless,
  And was sore wounded in that stour.

92. The reciter, from his advanced age, could not recollect the original line thus imperfectly supplied.—Ritson.

Also before that hour was done,
  Four of the thieves were slain,
Besides all those that wounded were,
  And eleven prisoners there was ta'en.

George Carrick, and his brother Edie,
  Them two, I wot they were both slain;
Harry Corbyl, and Lennie Carrick,
  Bore them company in their pain.

One of our Weardale-men was slain,
  Rowland Emerson his name hight;
I trust to God his soul is well,
  Because he 'fought' unto the right.

But thus they say'd, "We'll not depart
  While we have one:—speed back again!"
And when they came amongst the dead men,
  There they found George Carrick slain.

And when they found George Carrick slain,
  I wot it went well near their 'heart;'
Lord, let them never make a better end,
  That comes to play them sicken a 'part.'

I trust to God, no more they shall,
  Except it be one for a great chance;
For God will punish all those
  With a great heavy pestilence.

Thir limmer thieves, they have good hearts,
They nevir think to be o'erthrown;
Three banners against Weardale-men they bare,
As if the world had been all their own.

Thir Weardale-men, they have good hearts,
They are as stiff as any tree;
For, if they'd every one been slain,
Never a foot back man would flee.

And such a storm amongst them fell
As I think you never heard the like,
For he that bears his head so high,
He oft-times falls into the dyke.

And now I do entreat you all,
As many as are present here,
To pray for [the] singer of this song,
For he sings to make blithe your cheer.

THE RAID OF THE REIDSWIRE.

From *Minstrelsy of the Scottish Border*, ii. 15.

This ballad is preserved in the Bannatyne MS., and was first printed in Ramsay's *Evergreen*, ii. 224. Scott informs us that Ramsay took some liberties with the original text, and even interpolated the manuscript to favor his readings. A more accurate copy was given in the *Border Minstrelsy*. The text in Herd's

Scottish Songs, i. 91, and Caw's *Museum*, p. 235, is that of the *Evergreen*.

"The skirmish of the Reidswire happened upon the 7th of June, 1575, at one of the meetings held by the Wardens of the Marches, for arrangements necessary upon the Border. Sir John Carmichael was the Scottish Warden, and Sir John Forster held that office on the English Middle March. In the course of the day, which was employed as usual in redressing wrongs, a bill, or indictment, at the instance of a Scottish complainer, was fouled (*i. e.* found a true bill) against one Farnstein, a notorious English freebooter. Forster alleged that he had fled from justice. Carmichael, considering this as a pretext to avoid making compensation for the felony, bade him "play fair!" to which the haughty English warden retorted, by some injurious expressions respecting Carmichael's family, and gave other open signs of resentment. His retinue, chiefly men of Redesdale and Tynedale, the most ferocious of the English Borderers, glad of any pretext for a quarrel, discharged a flight of arrows among the Scots. A warm conflict ensued, in which, Carmichael being beat down and made prisoner, success seemed at first to incline to the English side, till the Tynedale men, throwing themselves too greedily upon the plunder, fell into disorder; and a body of Jedburgh citizens arriving at that instant, the skirmish terminated in a complete victory on the part of the Scots, who took prisoners, the English warden, James Ogle, Cuthbert Collingwood, Francis Russell, son to the Earl of Bedford, and son-in-law to Forster, some of the Fenwicks, and several other Border chiefs. They were sent to the Earl of Morton, then Regent, who detained them at Dalkeith for some days, till the heat of their resentment was abated; which prudent precaution prevented a war betwixt the two kingdoms. He then dismissed them with great expressions of regard; and, to satisfy Queen Elizabeth, sent Carmichael to York, whence he was soon after honourably dismissed. The field of battle, called the Reidswire, is a part of the Carter Mountain, about ten miles from Jedburgh."—SCOTT.

THE seventh of July, the suith to say,
At the Reidswire the tryst was set;
Our wardens they affixed the day,
And, as they promised, so they met.
Alas! that day I'll ne'er forgett!
Was sure sae feard, and then sae faine—
They came theare justice for to gett,
Will never green to come again.

Carmichael was our warden then,
He caused the country to conveen;
And the Laird's Wat, that worthie man,
Brought in that sirname weil beseen:
The Armestranges, that aye hae been
A hardy house, but not a hail,
The Elliots' honours to maintaine,
Brought down the lave o' Liddesdale.

2. *Swire* signifies the descent of a hill, and the epithet *Red* is derived from the color of the heath, or perhaps, from the Reid-water, which rises at no great distance.—S.

11. The Laird's Wat is perhaps the young Buccleuch, who, about twenty years after this *raid*, performed the great exploit of rescuing Kinmont Willie from Carlisle Castle.—S.

14. This clan are here mentioned as not being hail, or whole, because they were outlawed or broken men. Indeed, many of them had become Englishmen, as the phrase then

Then Tividale came to wi' spied;
The Sheriffe brought the Douglas down,
Wi' Cranstane, Gladstain, good at need,
Baith Rewle water, and Hawick town.
Beanjeddart bauldly made him boun,
Wi' a' the Trumbills, stronge and stout;
The Rutherfoords, with grit renown,
Convoy'd the town of Jedbrugh out.

Of other clans I cannot tell,
Because our warning was not wide—
Be this our folks hae ta'en the fell,
And planted down palliones, there to bide,
We looked down the other side,
And saw come breasting ower the brae,
Wi' Sir John Forster for their guyde,
Full fifteen hundred men and mae.

went. There was an old alliance betwixt the Elliots and Armstrongs, here alluded to.—S.

18. Douglas of Cavers, hereditary Sheriff of Teviotdale, descended from Black Archibald, who carried the standard of his father, the Earl of Douglas, at the battle of Otterbourne.—See the ballad of that name.—S.

24. These were ancient and powerful clans, residing chiefly upon the river Jed. Hence, they naturally convoyed the town of Jedburgh out. The following fragment of an old ballad is quoted in a letter from an aged gentleman of this name, residing at New York, to a friend in Scotland:—

"Bauld Rutherfurd, he was fou stout,
Wi' a' his nine sons him round about;
He led the town o' Jedburgh out,
All bravely fought that day.—S.

31. Sir John Forster, or, more properly, Forrester, of Balmbrough Abbey, Warden of the Middle Marches in 1561, was deputy-governor of Berwick, and governor of Balmborough Castle.—S.

It grieved him sair that day, I trow,
  Wi' Sir George Hearoune of Schipsydehouse;
Because we were not men enow,
  They counted us not worth a louse.
  Sir George was gentle, meek, and douse,
But *he* was hail and het as fire;
  And yet, for all his cracking crouse,
He rewd the raid o' the Reidswire.

To deal with proud men is but pain;
  For either must ye fight or flee,
Or else no answer make again,
  But play the beast, and let them be.
  It was na wonder he was hie,
Had Tindaill, Reedsdaill, at his hand,
  Wi' Cukdaill, Gladsdaill on the lee,
And Hebsrime, and Northumberland.

Yett was our meeting meek eneugh,
  Begun wi' merriment and mowes,
And at the brae, aboon the heugh,
  The clark sat down to call the rowes.
  And some for kyne, and some for ewes,
Call'd in of Dandrie, Hob, and Jock—

34. George Heron Miles of Chipchase Castle, probably the same who was slain at the Reidswire, was Sheriff of Northumberland, 13th Elizabeth.—S.

46. These are districts, or dales, on the English Border.

48. Mr. George Ellis suggests, with great probability, that this is a mistake, not for Hebburne, as the Editor stated in an earlier edition, but for Hexham, which, with its territory, formed a county independent of Northumberland, with which it is here ranked.—S.

We saw, come marching ower the knows,
Five hundred Fennicks in a flock,—

With jack and speir, and bows all bent,
And warlike weapons at their will:
Although we were na weel content,
Yet, by my troth, we fear'd no ill.
Some gaed to drink, and some stude still,
And some to cards and dice them sped;
Till on ane Farnstein they fyled a bill,
And he was fugitive and fled.

Carmichaell bade them speik out plainlie,
And cloke no cause for ill nor good;
The other, answering him as vainlie,
Began to reckon kin and blood:
He raise, and raxed him where he stood,
And bade him match him with his marrows;
Then Tindaill heard them reasun rude,
And they loot off a flight of arrows.

Then was there nought but bow and speir,
And every man pull'd out a brand;
"A Schafton and a Fenwick" thare:
Gude Symington was slain frae hand.
The Scotsmen cried on other to stand,
Frae time they saw John Robson slain—
What should they cry? the King's command
Could cause no cowards turn again.

56. The Fenwicks; a powerful and numerous Northumberland clan.—S.

Up rose the laird to red the cumber,
  Which would not be for all his boast;
What could we doe with sic a number—
  Fyve thousand men into a host?
  Then Henry Purdie proved his cost,
And very narrowlie had mischief'd him,
  And there we had our warden lost,
Wert not the grit God he relieved him.

Another throw the breiks him bair,
  Whill flatlies to the ground he fell:
Than thought I weel we had lost him there,
  Into my stomack it struck a knell!
  Yet up he raise, the treuth to tell ye,
And laid about him dints full dour;
  His horsemen they raid sturdily,
And stude about him in the stoure.

Then raise the slogan with ane shout—
  "Fy, Tindaill, to it! Jedburgh's here!"
I trow he was not half sae stout,
  But anis his stomach was asteir.

98. The gathering word peculiar to a certain name, or set of people, was termed *slogan* or *slughorn*, and was always repeated at an onset, as well as on many other occasions. It was usually the name of the clan, or place of rendezvous, or leader. In 1335, the English, led by Thomas of Rosslyne, and William Moubray, assaulted Aberdeen. The former was mortally wounded in the onset; and, as his followers were pressing forward, shouting "*Rosslyne! Rosslyne!*" "Cry *Moubray*," said the expiring chieftain; "*Rosslyne* is gone!"—S.

With gun and genzie, bow and speir,
Men might see mony a cracked crown!
But up amang the merchant geir,
They were as busy as we were down.

The swallow taill frae tackles flew,
Five hundredth flain into a flight:
But we had pestelets enew,
And shot among them as we might.
With help of God the game gaed right,
Fra time the foremost of them fell;
Then ower the know, without goodnight,
They ran with mony a shout and yell.

But after they had turned backs,
Yet Tindail men they turn'd again,
And had not been the merchant packs,
There had been mae of Scotland slain.
But, Jesu! if the folks were fain
To put the bussing on their thies;
And so they fled, wi' a' their main,
Down ower the brae, like clogged bees.

Sir Francis Russell ta'en was there,
And hurt, as we hear men rehearse;

115. The ballad-maker here ascribes the victory to the real cause; for the English Borderers dispersing to plunder the merchandise, gave the opposite party time to recover from their surprise. It seems to have been usual for travelling merchants to attend Border meetings, although one would have thought the kind of company usually assembled there might have deterred them.—S.

121. This gentleman was son to the Earl of Bedford, and

Proud Wallinton was wounded sair,
Albeit he be a Fennick fierce.
But if ye wald a souldier search,
Among them a' were ta'en that night,
Was nane sae wordie to put in verse,
As Collingwood, that courteous knight.

Young Henry Schafton, he is hurt;
A souldier shot him wi' a bow;
Scotland has cause to mak great sturt,
For laiming of the Laird of Mow.
The Laird's Wat did weel indeed;
His friends stood stoutlie by himsell,
With little Gladstain, gude in need,
For Gretein kend na gude be ill.

The Sheriffe wanted not gude will,
Howbeit he might not fight so fast;
Beanjeddart, Hundlie, and Hunthill,

Varden of the East Marches. He was, at this time, cham-erlain of Berwick.—S.

123. Fenwick of Wallington, a powerful Northumbrian hief.—S.

128. Sir Cuthbert Collingwood of Esslington, Sheriff of Jorthumberland, the 10th and 20th of Elizabeth.—S.

129. The Shaftoes are an ancient family settled at Baving-on, in Northumberland, since the time of Edward I.—S.

132. An ancient family on the Borders. The Laird of Aowe here mentioned was the only gentleman of note killed n the skirmish on the Scottish side.—S.

136. Graden, a family of Kers.—S.

139. Douglas of Beanjeddart, an ancient branch of the 1ouse of Cavers, possessing property near the junction of

Three, on they laid weel at the last.
Except the horsemen of the guard,
If I could put men to availe,
None stoutlier stood out for their laird,
Nor did the lads of Liddisdail.

But little harness had we there;
But auld Badreule had on a jack,
And did right weel, I you declare,
With all his Trumbills at his back.
Gude Edderstane was not to lack,
Nor Kirktoun, Newton, noble men!
Thir's all the specials I of speake,
By others that I could not ken.

Who did invent that day of play,
We need not fear to find him soon;

the Jed and Teviot. *Hundlie.*—Rutherford of Hundlie, or Hundalee, situated on the Jed above Jedburgh. *Hunthill.*—The old tower of Hunthill was situated about a mile above Jedburgh. It was the patrimony of an ancient family of Rutherfords. I suppose the person, here meant, to be the same who is renowned in tradition by the name of the *Cock of Hunthill.*—S.

146. Sir Andrew Turnbull of Bedrule, upon Rule Water. —S.

149. An ancient family of Rutherfords; I believe, indeed, the most ancient now extant.—S.

150. The parish of Kirktoun belonged, I believe, about this time, to a branch of the Cavers family; but Kirkton of Stewartfield is mentioned in the list of Border clans in 1597. *Newton.*—This is probably Grinyslaw of Little Newton, mentioned in the said roll of Border clans.—S.

For Sir John Forster, I dare well say,
  Made us this noisome afternoon.
  Not that I speak preceislie out,
That he supposed it would be perril;
  But pride, and breaking out of feuid,
Garr'd Tindaill lads begin the quarrel.

THE DEATH OF PARCY REED.

TAKEN down from the recitation of an old woman, and first published (certainly not without what are called "improvements") in Richardson's *Borderer's Table Book*, vol. vii. p. 364, with an introduction by Mr. Robert White, which we here abridge.

Percival or Parcy Reed, was proprietor of Troughend, a tract of land in Redesdale, Northumberland, a man of courage and devoted to the chase. Having been appointed warden of the district, he had the misfortune in the discharge of his duties, to offend a family of the name of Hall, who were owners of the farm of Girsonsfield, and also to incur the enmity of a band of moss-troopers, Crosier by name, some of whom had been brought to justice by his hands. The Halls concealed their resentment until they were able to contrive an opportunity for taking a safe revenge.

In pursuance of this design, they requested Reed to join them on a hunting party. Their invitation was unsuspiciously accepted, and after a day of sport the company retired to a solitary hut in the lonely glen of Batinghope. Here Reed was attacked in the evening by the Crosiers, and as the Halls not only refused their assistance, but had treacherously deprived him of the means of defence by rendering his sword and gun unserviceable, he fell an easy victim to his savage foes.

It is probable that we cannot assign to the event on which this piece is founded, a date later than the sixteenth century.

The story of Parcy Reed is alluded to in *Rokeby*, canto first, xx.; Sir Walter Scott has also taken the death of his dog Keeldar as the subject of a poem contributed to Hood's annual, *The Gem*, for 1829.

GOD send the land deliverance
  Frae every reaving, riding Scot;
We'll sune hae neither cow nor ewe,
  We'll sune hae neither staig nor stot.

The outlaws come frae Liddesdale,
  They herry Redesdale far and near;
The rich man's gelding it maun gang,
  They canna pass the puir man's mear.

Sure it were weel, had ilka thief
  Around his neck a halter strang;
And curses heavy may they light
  On traitors vile oursels amang.

Now Parcy Reed has Crosier ta'en,
He has delivered him to the law ;
But Crosier says he'll do waur than that,
He'll make the tower o' Troughend fa'.

And Crosier says he will do waur—
He will do waur if waur can be ;
He'll make the bairns a' fatherless ;
And then, the land it may lie lee.

"To the hunting, ho !" cried Parcy Reed,
"The morning sun is on the dew ;
The cauler breeze frae off the fells
Will lead the dogs to the quarry true.

"To the hunting, ho !" cried Parcy Reed,
And to the hunting he has gane ;
And the three fause Ha's o' Girsonsfield
Alang wi' him he has them ta'en.

They hunted high, they hunted low,
By heathery hill and birken shaw ;
They raised a buck on Rooken Edge,
And blew the mort at fair Ealylawe.

They hunted high, they hunted low,
They made the echoes ring amain ;
With music sweet o' horn and hound,
They merry made fair Redesdale glen.

They hunted high, they hunted low,
  They hunted up, they hunted down,
Until the day was past the prime,
  And it grew late in the afternoon.

They hunted high in Batinghope,
  When as the sun was sinking low,
Says Parcy then, "Ca' off the dogs,
  We'll bait our steeds and homeward go."

They lighted high in Batinghope,
  Atween the brown and benty ground;
They had but rested a little while,
  Till Parcy Reed was sleeping sound.

There's nane may lean on a rotten staff,
  But him that risks to get a fa';
There's nane may in a traitor trust,
  And traitors black were every Ha'.

They've stown the bridle off his steed,
  And they've put water in his lang gun;
They've fixed his sword within the sheath,
  That out again it winna come.

"Awaken ye, waken ye, Parcy Reed,
  Or by your enemies be ta'en;
For yonder are the five Crosiers
  A-coming owre the Hingin-stane."

"If they be five, and we be four,
Sae that ye stand alang wi' me,
Then every man ye will take one,
And only leave but two to me:
We will them meet as brave men ought,
And make them either fight or flee."

"We mayna stand, we canna stand,
We daurna stand alang wi' thee;
The Crosiers haud thee at a feud,
And they wad kill baith thee and we."

"O, turn thee, turn thee, Johnie Ha',
O, turn thee, man, and fight wi' me;
When ye come to Troughend again,
My gude black naig I will gie thee;
He cost full twenty pound o' gowd,
Atween my brother John and me."

"I mayna turn, I canna turn,
I daurna turn and fight wi' thee;
The Crosiers haud thee at a feud,
And they wad kill baith thee and me."

"O, turn thee, turn thee, Willie Ha',
O, turn thee, man, and fight wi' me;
When ye come to Troughend again,
A yoke o' owsen I'll gie thee."

"I mayna turn, I canna turn,
I daurna turn and fight wi' thee;

The Crosiers haud thee at a feud,
  And they wad kill baith thee and me."

"O, turn thee, turn thee, Tommy Ha',
  O, turn now, man, and fight wi' me;
If ever we come to Troughend again,
  My daughter Jean I'll gie to thee."

"I mayna turn, I canna turn,
  I daurna turn and fight wi' thee;
The Crosiers haud thee at a feud,
  And they wad kill baith thee and me."

"O, shame upon ye, traitors a'!
  I wish your hames ye may never see;
Ye've stown the bridle off my naig,
  And I can neither fight nor flee.

"Ye've stown the bridle off my naig,
  And ye've put water i' my lang gun;
Ye've fixed my sword within the sheath,
  That out again it winna come."

He had but time to cross himsel',
  A prayer he hadna time to say,
Till round him came the Crosiers keen,
  All riding graithed, and in array.

"Weel met, weel met, now, Parcy Reed,
  Thou art the very man we sought;

Owre lang hae we been in your debt,
  Now will we pay you as we ought.

"We'll pay thee at the nearest tree,
  Where we shall hang thee like a hound;"
Brave Parcy rais'd his fankit sword,
  And fell'd the foremost to the ground.

Alake, and wae for Parcy Reed,
  Alake, he was an unarmed man;
Four weapons pierced him all at once,
  As they assailed him there and than.

They fell upon him all at once,
  They mangled him most cruellie;
The slightest wound might caused his deid,
  And they have gi'en him thirty-three.
They hacket off his hands and feet,
  And left him lying on the lee.

"Now, Parcy Reed, we've paid our debt,
  Ye canna weel dispute the tale,"
The Crosiers said, and off they rade—
  They rade the airt o' Liddesdale.

It was the hour o' gloamin' gray,
  When herds come in frae fauld and pen;
A herd he saw a huntsman lie,
  Says he, "Can this be Laird Troughen'?"

"There's some will ca' me Parcy Reed,
And some will ca' me Laird Troughen';
It's little matter what they ca' me,
My faes hae made me ill to ken.

"There's some will ca' me Parcy Reed,
And speak my praise in tower and town;
It's little matter what they do now,
My life-blood rudds the heather brown.

"There's some will ca' me Parcy Reed,
And a' my virtues say and sing;
I would much rather have just now
A draught o' water frae the spring!"

The herd flung aff his clouted shoon,
And to the nearest fountain ran;
He made his bonnet serve a cup,
And wan the blessing o' the dying man.

"Now, honest herd, ye maun do mair,—
Ye maun do mair as I ye tell;
Ye maun bear tidings to Troughend,
And bear likewise my last farewell.

"A farewell to my wedded wife,
A farewell to my brother John,
Wha sits into the Troughend tower,
Wi' heart as black as any stone.

"A farewell to my daughter Jean,
  A farewell to my young sons five;
Had they been at their father's hand,
  I had this night been man alive.

"A farewell to my followers a',
  And a' my neighbours gude at need;
Bid them think how the treacherous Ha's
  Betrayed the life o' Parcy Reed.

"The laird o' Clennel bears my bow,
  The laird o' Brandon bears my brand;
Whene'er they ride i' the border side,
  They'll mind the fate o' the laird Troughend."

CAPTAIN CAR, OR, EDOM O' GORDON.

"This ballad is founded upon a real event, which took place in the north of Scotland in the year 1571, during the struggles between the party which held out for the imprisoned Queen Mary, and that which endeavoured to maintain the authority of her infant son, James VI. The person designated Edom o' Gordon was Adam Gordon of Auchindown, brother of the Marquis of Huntly, and his deputy as lieutenant of the north of Scotland for the Queen. This gentleman committed many acts of oppression on the clan Forbes, under colour of the Queen's authority, and in one collision with that family, killed Arthur, brother to Lord Forbes. He afterwards sent a party under one Captain Car, or Ker, to reduce the house of Towie, one of the chief seats of the name of Forbes. The proprietor of the mansion being from home, his lady, who was pregnant at the time, confiding too much in her sex and condition, not only refused to surrender, but gave Car some very opprobious language over the walls, which irritated him so much that he set fire to the house, and burnt the whole inmates, amounting in all to thirty-seven persons. As Gordon never cashiered Car for this inhuman action, he was held by the public voice to be equally guilty, and accordingly [in one of the versions of the ballad] he is represented as the principal actor himself." (CHAMBERS'S *Scottish Ballads*, p. 67.) It appears that the Forbeses afterwards attempted to assassinate Adam Gordon in the streets of Paris. See more of this Captain Ker under *The Battell of Balrinnes*, in the next volume.

The ballad was first printed by the Foulises at Glasgow, 1755, under the title of *Edom of Gordon*, as taken down by Sir David Dalrymple from the recitation of a lady. It was inserted in the *Reliques*, (i. 122,) "improved and enlarged," (or, as Ritson more correctly expresses the fact, "interpolated and corrupted,") by several stanzas from a fragment in Percy's manuscript, called *Captain Adam Carre*. Ritson published the following genuine and ancient copy, (*Ancient Songs*, ii. 38,) from a collection in the Cotton Library. He states that his MS. had received numerous alterations or corrections, all or most of which, as being evidently for the better, he had adopted into the text. We have added a copy of

Edom o' Gordon given in Ritson's *Scottish Songs*, and in the Appendix an inferior version of the story, called *Loudoun Castle.*

The names vary considerably in the different versions of this piece. The castle of Towie, or the house of Rothes, is here called the castle of Crecrynbroghe, in Percy's manuscript the castle of Brittonsborrow, and in the copy in the Appendix the locality is changed to Loudoun castle in Ayrshire. In like manner, Alexander Forbes is here turned into Lord Hamleton, and Captain Car is now called the lord of Easter-town and again the lord of Westerton-town.

In the *Gentleman's Magazine*, vol. xci. Part 1, p. 451, will be found a modern ballad styled *Adam Gordon*, founded on the adventure of the freebooter of that name with Edward the First. Another on the same subject is given in Evans's *Old Ballads*, iv. 86.

It befell at Martynmas
When wether waxed colde,
Captaine Care saide to his men,
"We must go take a holde."

"Haille, master, and wether you will,
And wether ye like it best."
"To the castle of Crecrynbroghe;
And there we will take our reste.

"I knowe wher is a gay castle,
Is build of lyme and stone,
Within 'there' is a gay ladie,
Her lord is ryd from hom."

The ladie lend on her castle-walle,
She loked upp and downe;
There was she ware of an host of men,
Come riding to the towne.

"Come yow hether, my meri men all,
And look what I do see;
Yonder is ther an host of men,
I musen who they bee."

She thought he had been her own wed lord,
That had comd riding home;
Then was it traitour Captaine Care,
The lord of Ester-towne.

They were no soner at supper sett,
Then after said the grace,
Or captaine Care and all his men
Wer lighte aboute the place.

"Gyve over thi howsse, thou lady gay,
And I will make the a bande;
To-nighte thoust ly wythin my arm,
To-morrowe thou shall ere my lan[de]."

Then bespacke the eldest sonne,
That was both whitt and redde,
"O mother dere, geve over your howsse,
Or elles we shal be deade."

"I will not geve over my hous," she saithe,
"Not for feare of my lyffe;
It shal be talked throughout the land,
The slaughter of a wyffe.

"Fetch me my pestilett,
And charge me my gonne,
That I may shott at the bloddy butcher,
The lord of Easter-towne."

She styfly stod on her castle-wall,
And lett the pellettes flee,
She myst the blody bucher,
And slew other three.

"I will not geve over my hous," she saithe,
"Netheir for lord nor lowne,
Nor yet for traitour Captaine Care,
The lord of Easter-towne.

"I desire of Captaine Care,
And all his bloddye band,
That he would save my eldest sonne,
The eare of all my lande."

"Lap him in a shete," he sayth,
"And let him downe to me,
And I shall take him in my armes,
His waran wyll I be."

The captayne sayd unto himselfe,
Wyth sped before the rest;
He cut his tonge out of his head,
His hart out of his brest.

He lapt them in a handerchef,
And knet it of knotes three,
And cast them over the castell-wall
At that gay ladye.

" Fye upon thee, Captaine Care,
And all thy bloddy band,
For thou hast slayne my eldest sonne,
The ayre of all my land."

Then bespake the yongest sonn,
That sat on the nurses knee,
Sayth, " Mother gay, geve ower your house,
[The smoke] it smoldereth me."

" I wold geve my gold," she saith,
" And so I wolde my fee,
For a blaste of the wesleyn wind
To dryve the smoke from thee.

" Fy upon thee, John Hamleton,
That ever I paid thé hyre,
For thou hast broken my castle-wall,
And kyndled in [it] the fyre."

84, thee.

The lady gate to her close parler,
  The fire fell aboute her head;
She toke up her children thre,
  Seth, "Babes, we are all dead."

Then bespake the hye steward,
  That is of hye degree;
Saith, "Ladie gay, you are no 'bote,'
  Wethere ye fighte or flee."

Lord Hamleton dremd in his dreame,
  In Carvall where he laye,
His halle 'was' all of fyre,
  His ladie slayne or daye.

"Busk and bowne, my merry men all,
  Even and go ye with me,
For I 'dremd' that my hall was on fyre
  My lady slayne or day."

He buskt him and bownd him,
  And like a worthi knighte,
And when he saw his hall burning,
  His harte was no dele lighte.

He sett a trumpett till his mouth,
  He blew as it plesd his grace;
Twenty score of Hambletons
  Was light aboute the place.

"Had I knowne as much yesternighte
As I do to-daye,
Captaine Care and all his men
Should not have gone so quite [awaye.]

"Fye upon thee, Captaine Care,
And all thy blody 'bande;'
Thou hast slayne my lady gaye,
More worth then all thy lande.

"Yf thou had ought eny ill will," he saith,
"Thou shoulde have taken my lyffe,
And have saved my children thre,
All and my lovesome wyffe."

EDOM O' GORDON.

From Ritson's *Scottish Songs*, ii. 17. We presume this is the ballad printed by the Foulises.

It fell about the Martinmas,
Quhen the wind blew schrile and cauld,
Said Edom o' Gordon to his men,
"We maun draw to a hauld.

"And what an a hauld sall we draw to,
My merry men and me?
We will gae to the house of the Rodes,
To see that fair ladie."

She had nae sooner busket hersell,
Nor putten on her gown,
Till Edom o' Gordon and his men
Were round about the town.

They had nae sooner sitten down,
Nor sooner said the grace,
Till Edom o' Gordon and his men
Were closed about the place.

The lady ran up to her tower head,
As fast as she could drie,
To see if by her fair speeches,
She could with him agree.

As soon as he saw the lady fair,
And hir yates all locked fast,
He fell into a rage of wrath,
And his heart was aghast.

"Cum down to me, ze lady fair,
Cum down to me, let's see;
This night ze's ly by my ain side,
The morn my bride sall be."

"I winnae cum down, ye fals Gordon,
I winnae cum down to thee;
I winnae forsake my ane dear lord
That is sae far frae me."

24. heart, *pronounced* hearrut.

"Gi up your house, ze fair lady,
  Gi up your house to me,
Or I will burn zoursel therein,
  Bot you and zour babies three."

"I winna gie up, zou fals Gordon,
  To nae sik traitor as thee,
Tho' zou should burn mysel therein,
  Bot and my babies three."

"Set fire to the house," quoth fals Gordon,
  "Sin better may nae bee;
And I will burn hersel therein,
  Bot and her babies three."

"And ein wae worth ze, Jock my man,
  I paid ze weil zour fee;
Why pow ze out my ground wa' stane,
  Lets in the reek to me?

"And ein wae worth ze, Jock my man,
  For I paid zou weil zour hire;
Why pow ze out my ground wa' stane,
  To me lets in the fire?"

"Ye paid me weil my hire, lady,
  Ye paid me weil my fee,
But now I'm Edom of Gordon's man,
  Maun either do or die."

O then bespake her zoungest son,
Sat on the nurses knee,
"Dear mother, gie owre your house," he says,
"For the reek it worries me."

"I winnae gie up my house, my dear,
To nae sik traitor as he;
Cum well, cum wae, my jewels fair,
Ye maun tak share wi me."

O then bespake her dochter dear,
She was baith jimp and sma,
"O row me in a pair o' shiets,
And tow me owre the wa."

They rowd her in a pair of shiets,
And towd her owre the wa,
But, on the point of Edom's speir,
She gat a deadly fa'.

O bonny, bonny, was hir mouth,
And chirry were her cheiks,
And clear, clear was hir zellow hair,
Whereon the reid bluid dreips.

Then wi his speir he turn'd hir owr,
O gin hir face was wan!
He said, "Zou are the first that eer
I wisht alive again."

He turn'd her owr and owr again;
  O gin hir skin was whyte!
He said, "I might ha spard thy life,
  To been some mans delyte."

"Busk and boon, my merry men all,
  For ill dooms I do guess;
I cannae luik in that bonny face,
  As it lyes on the grass."

"Them luiks to freits, my master deir,
  Their freits will follow them;
Let it neir be said brave Edom o' Gordon
  Was daunted with a dàme."

O then he spied hir ain deir lord,
  As he came owr the lee;
He saw his castle in a fire,
  As far as he could see.

"Put on, put on, my mighty men,
  As fast as ze can drie,
For he that's hindmost of my men,
  Sall neir get guid o' me."

And some they raid, and some they ran,
  Fu fast out owr the plain,
But lang, lang, eer he coud get up,
  They were a' deid and slain.

90. Then. 97. *Qy.* wight yemen?

But mony were the mudie men
  Lay gasping on the grien;
For o' fifty men that Edom brought out
  There were but five ged heme.

And mony were the mudie men
  Lay gasping on the grien,
And mony were the fair ladys
  Lay lemanless at heme.

And round and round the waes he went,
  Their ashes for to view;
At last into the flames he flew,
  And bad the world adieu.

WILLIE MACKINTOSH, OR, THE BURNING OF AUCHINDOWN.

THESE fragments appear to relate to the burning of Auchindown, a castle belonging to the Gordons, in vengeance for the death of William Mackintosh of the clan Chattan, which is said to have occurred at the castle of the Earl of Huntly. The event is placed in the year 1592. After the Mackintoshes had executed their revenge, they were pursued by the Gordons, and overtaken in the Stapler, where "sixty of the clan Chattan were killed, and Willie Mackintosh, their leader, wounded." So says the not very trustworthy editor of the *Thistle of Scotland.*

Another fragment of four stanzas (containing nothing additional), is given by Whitelaw, *Book of Scottish Ballads*, p. 248.

I.

From Finlay's *Scottish Ballads*, ii. 97.

As I came in by Fiddich-side,
In a May morning,
I met Willie Mackintosh
An hour before the dawning.

"Turn again, turn again,
Turn again, I bid ye;
If ye burn Auchindown,
Huntly he will head ye."

"Head me, hang me,
That sall never fear me;
I'll burn Auchindown
Before the life leaves me."

As I came in by Auchindown,
In a May morning,
Auchindown was in a bleeze,
An hour before the dawning.

* * * * *

"Crawing, crawing,
For my crowse crawing,
I lost the best feather i' my wing,
For my crowse crawing."

II.

From *The Thistle of Scotland*, p. 106.

"Turn, Willie Mackintosh,
Turn, I bid you,
Gin ye burn Auchindown,
Huntly will head you."

"Head me, or hang me,
That canna fley me,
I'll burn Auchindown,
Ere the life lea' me."

Coming down Dee-side
In a clear morning,
Auchindown was in a flame,
Ere the cock crawing.

But coming o'er Cairn Croom,
And looking down, man,
I saw Willie Mackintosh
Burn Auchindown, man.

"Bonny Willie Mackintosh,
Whare left ye your men?"
"I left them in the Stapler,
But they'll never come hame."

"Bonny Willie Mackintosh,
Where now is your men?"
"I left them in the Stapler,
Sleeping in their sheen."

LORD MAXWELL'S GOODNIGHT.

Minstrelsy of the Scottish Border, ii. 199.

"A. D. 1585, John Lord Maxwell, or, as he styled himself, Earl of Morton, having quarrelled with the Earl of Arran, reigning favourite of James VI., and fallen, of course, under the displeasure of the court, was denounced rebel. A commission was also given to the Laird of Johnstone, then Warden of the West Marches, to pursue and apprehend the ancient rival and enemy of his house. Two bands of mercenaries, commanded by Captains Cranstoun and Lammie, who were sent from Edinburgh to support Johnstone, were attacked and cut to pieces at Crawford-muir, by Robert Maxwell, natural brother to the chieftain; who, following up his advantage, burned Johnstone's

Castle of Lochwood, observing, with savage glee, that he would give Lady Johnstone light enough by which 'to set her hood.' In a subsequent conflict, Johnstone himself was defeated, and made prisoner, and is said to have died of grief at the disgrace which he sustained.

"By one of the revolutions, common in those days, Maxwell was soon after restored to the King's favour in his turn, and obtained the wardenry of the West Marches. A bond of alliance was subscribed by him, and by Sir James Johnstone, and for some time the two clans lived in harmony. In the year 1593, however, the hereditary feud was revived on the following occasion. A band of marauders, of the clan Johnstone, drove a prey of cattle from the lands belonging to the Lairds of Crichton, Sanquhar, and Drumlanrig; and defeated, with slaughter, the pursuers, who attempted to rescue their property.—[See *The Lads of Wamphray*, post, p. 168.] The injured parties, being apprehensive that Maxwell would not cordially embrace their cause, on account of his late reconciliation with the Johnstones, endeavoured to overcome his reluctance, by offering to enter into bonds of manrent, and so to become his followers and liegemen; he, on the other hand, granting to them a bond of maintenance, or protection, by which he bound himself, in usual form, to maintain their quarrel against all mortals, saving his loyalty. Thus, the most powerful and respectable families in Dumfriesshire, became, for a time, the vassals of Lord Maxwell. This secret alliance was discovered to Sir James Johnstone by the Laird of Cummertrees, one of his own clan, though a retainer to Maxwell. Cummertrees even contrived to possess himself of the bonds of manrent, which he delivered to his chief. The petty warfare betwixt the rival barons was instantly renewed. Buccleuch, a near relation of Johnstone, came to his assistance with his clan, 'the most renowned freebooters, [says a historian,] the fiercest and bravest warriors among the Border tribes.' With Buccleuch also came the Elliots, Armstrongs, and Græmes. Thus reinforced, Johnstone surprised and cut to pieces a party of the Maxwells, stationed at Lochmaben. On the other hand, Lord Maxwell, armed with the royal authority, and numbering among his followers all the barons of Nithsdale, displayed his banner as the King's lieutenant, and invaded Annandale at the head of two thousand men. In those days, however, the royal auspices seem to have carried as little good fortune as effective strength with them. A desperate conflict, still renowned in tradition, took place at the Dryffe Sands, not far from Lockerby, in which Johnstone, although inferior in numbers, partly by his own conduct, partly by the valour of his allies, gained a decisive victory. Lord Maxwell, a tall man, and heavily armed, was struck from his horse in the flight, and cruelly slain, after the hand, which he stretched out for quarter, had been severed from his body. Many of his followers were slain in the battle, and many cruelly wounded, especially by slashes in the face, which wound was thence termed a 'Lockerby lick.' The Barons of Lag, Closeburn, and Drumlanrig, escaped by the fleetness of their horses; a circumstance alluded to in the following ballad.

"John, Lord Maxwell, with whose 'Goodnight' the reader is here presented, was son to him who fell at the battle of Dryffe Sands, and is said to have early avowed the deepest revenge for his father's death. Such, indeed, was the fiery and untameable spirit of the man, that neither the threats nor entreaties of the King himself could make him lay aside his vindictive purpose; although Johnstone, the object of his resentment, had not only reconciled himself to the court, but even obtained the wardenry of the Middle Marches, in room of Sir John Carmichael, murdered by the Armstrongs. Lord Maxwell was therefore prohibited to approach the Border counties; and having, in contempt of that mandate, excited new disturbances, he was confined in the castle of Edinburgh. From this fortress, however, he contrived to make his escape; and, having repaired to Dumfriesshire, he sought an amicable interview with Johnstone, under a pretence of a wish to accommodate their differences. Sir Robert Maxwell, of Orchardstane, (mentioned in the ballad, verse 1,) who was married to a sister of Sir James Johnstone, persuaded his brother-in-law to accede to Maxwell's proposal."

So far Sir Walter Scott. The meeting took place on the 6th of April, 1608, in the presence of Sir Robert Maxwell, each party being accompanied by a single follower. While the chieftains were conferring together, Charles Maxwell, the attendant of Lord John, maliciously began an altercation with the servant of Johnstone, and shot him with a pistol, and Sir James, looking round at the report, was himself shot by Lord Maxwell in the back with two poisoned bullets.

The murderer escaped to France, but afterwards venturing to return to Scotland, was apprehended, brought to trial at Edinburgh, and beheaded on the 21st of May, 1613. We may naturally suppose that the *Goodnight* was composed shortly after Lord Maxwell fled across the seas, certainly before 1613.

This ballad was first printed in the *Border Minstrelsy* "from a copy in Glenriddel's MSS., with some slight variations from tradition."

"Adieu, madame, my mother dear,
 But and my sisters three!
Adieu, fair Robert of Orchardstane!
 My heart is wae for thee.
Adieu, the lily and the rose,
 The primrose fair to see!
Adieu, my ladye, and only joy!
 For I may not stay with thee.

" Though I hae slain the Lord Johnstone,
 What care I for their feid?
My noble mind their wrath disdains,—
 He was my father's deid.
Both night and day I labour'd oft
 Of him avenged to be;
But now I've got what lang I sought,
 And I may not stay with thee.

"Adieu, Drumlanrig! false wert aye—
 And Closeburn in a band!
The Laird of Lag, frae my father that fled,
 When the Johnston struck aff his hand!

They were three brethren in a band—
Joy may they never see!
Their treacherous art, and cowardly heart,
Has twined my love and me.

"Adieu, Dumfries, my proper place,
But and Carlaverock fair!
Adieu, my castle of the Thrieve,
Wi' a' my buildings there!
Adieu, Lochmaben's gate sae fair,
The Langholm-holm, where birks there be!
Adieu, my ladye, and only joy!
For, trust me, I may not stay wi' thee.

"Adieu, fair Eskdale, up and down,
Where my puir friends do dwell!
The bangisters will ding them down,
And will them sair compell.
But I'll avenge their feid mysell,
When I come o'er the sea;
Adieu, my ladye, and only joy!
For I may not stay wi' thee."

" Lord of the land,"—that ladye said,
" O wad ye go wi' me,
Unto my brother's stately tower,
Where safest ye may be!
There Hamiltons, and Douglas baith,
Shall rise to succour thee."
" Thanks for thy kindness, fair my dame,
But I may not stay wi' thee."

Then he tuik aff a gay gold ring,
  Thereat hang signets three;
"Hae, tak thee that, mine ain dear thing,
  And still hae mind o' me:
But if thou take another lord,
  Ere I come ower the sea—
His life is but a three days' lease,
  Though I may not stay wi' thee."

The wind was fair, the ship was clear,
  That good lord went away;
And most part of his friends were there,
  To give him a fair convey.
They drank the wine, they didna spair,
  Even in that gude lord's sight—
Sae now he's o'er the floods sae gray,
  And Lord Maxwell has ta'en his Goodnight.

THE LADS OF WAMPHRAY

Minstrelsy of the Scottish Border, ii. 148.

"The reader will find, prefixed to the foregoing ballad, an account of the noted feud betwixt the families of Maxwell and Johnstone. The following song celebrates the skirmish, in 1593, betwixt the Johnstones and Crichtons, which led to the revival of the ancient quarrel betwixt Johnstone and Maxwell, and finally to the battle of Dryffe Sands, in which the latter lost his life. Wamphray is the name of a parish in Annandale. Lethenhall was the abode of Johnstone of Wamphray, and continued to be so till of late years. William Johnstone of Wamphray, called the Galliard, was a noted freebooter. A place, near the head of Teviotdale, retains the name of the Galliard's Faulds, (folds,) being a valley, where he used to secrete and divide his spoil, with his Liddesdale and Eskdale associates. His *nom de guerre* seems to have been derived from the dance called the Galliard. The word is still used in Scotland, to express an active, gay, dissipated character. Willie of the Kirkhill, nephew to the Galliard, and his avenger, was also a noted Border robber. Previous to the battle of Dryffe Sands, so often mentioned, tradition reports, that Maxwell had offered a ten-pound-land to any of his party, who should bring him the head or hand of the Laird of Johnstone. This being reported to his antagonist, he answered, he had not a ten-pound-land to offer, but would give a five-merk-land to the man who should that day cut off the head or hand of Lord Maxwell. Willie of the Kirkhill, mounted upon a young grey horse, rushed upon the enemy, and earned the reward, by striking down their unfortunate chieftain, and cutting off his right hand."—SCOTT.

'TWIXT Girth-head and the Langwood end,
Lived the Galliard, and the Galliard's men,
But and the lads of Leverhay,
That drove the Crichton's gear away.

1-7. Leverhay, Stefenbiggin, Girth-head, &c., are all situated in the parish of Wamphray.—S.

It is the lads of Lethenha',
The greatest rogues amang them a';
But and the lads of Stefenbiggin,
They broke the house in at the rigging.

The lads of Fingland, and Helbeck-hill,
They were never for good, but aye for ill;
'Twixt the Staywood-bush and Langside-hill,
They steal'd the broked cow and the branded bull.

It is the lads of the Girth-head,
The deil's in them for pride and greed;
For the Galliard, and the gay Galliard's men,
They ne'er saw a horse but they made it their ain.

The Galliard to Nithsdale is gane,
To steal Sim Crichton's winsome dun;
The Galliard is unto the stable gane,
But instead of the dun, the blind he has ta'en.

"Now Simmy, Simmy of the Side,
Come out and see a Johnstone ride!
Here's the bonniest horse in a' Nithside,
And a gentle Johnstone aboon his hide."

Simmy Crichton's mounted then,
And Crichtons has raised mony a ane;
The Galliard trow'd his horse had been wight,
But the Crichtons beat him out o' sight.

As soon as the Galliard the Crichton saw,
Behind the saugh-bush he did draw;
And there the Crichtons the Galliard hae ta'en,
And nane wi' him but Willie alane.

"O Simmy, Simmy, now let me gang,
And I'll never mair do a Crichton wrang!
O Simmy, Simmy, now let me be,
And a peck o' gowd I'll give to thee!

"O Simmy, Simmy, now let me gang,
And my wife shall heap it with her hand!"
But the Crichtons wadna let the Galliard be,
But they hang'd him hie upon a tree.

O think then Willie he was right wae,
When he saw his uncle guided sae;
"But if ever I live Wamphray to see,
My uncle's death avenged shall be!"

Back to Wamphray he is gane,
And riders has raised mony a ane;
Saying—"My lads, if ye'll be true,
Ye shall a' be clad in the noble blue."

Back to Nithsdale they have gane,
And awa' the Crichtons' nowt hae ta'en;
But when they cam to the Wellpath-head,
The Crichtons bade them light and lead.

51-53. The Wellpath is a pass by which the Johnstones

And when they cam to the Biddes-burn,
The Crichtons bade them stand and turn;
And when they cam to the Biddes-strand,
The Crichtons they were hard at hand.

But when they cam to the Biddes-law,
The Johnstones bade them stand and draw;
"We've done nae ill, we'll thole nae wrang,
But back to Wamphray we will gang."

And out spoke Willie of the Kirkhill,
"Of fighting, lads, ye'se hae your fill;"
And from his horse Willie he lap,
And a burnish'd brand in his hand he gat.

Out through the Crichtons Willie he ran,
And dang them down baith horse and man;
O but the Johnstones were wondrous rude,
When the Biddes-burn ran three days blood!

"Now, sirs, we have done a noble deed,—
We have revenged the Galliard's bleid;
For every finger of the Galliard's hand,
I vow this day I've kill'd a man."

were retreating to their fastnesses in Annandale. The Biddes-burn, where the skirmish took place betwixt the Johnstones and their pursuers, is a rivulet which takes its course among the mountains on the confines of Nithesdale and Annandale.—S.

As they cam in at Evan-head,
At Ricklaw-holm they spread abread;
"Drive on, my lads! it will be late;
We'll hae a pint at Wamphray gate.

"For where'er I gang, or e'er I ride,
The lads of Wamphray are on my side;
And of a' the lads that I do ken,
A Wamphray lad's the king of men."

THE FIRE OF FRENDRAUGHT.

From Motherwell's *Minstrelsy*, p. 161.

"A MORTAL feud having arisen between the Laird of Frendraught [Sir James Chrichton] and the Laird of Rothiemay [William Gordon], both gentlemen of Banffshire, a rencontre took place, at which the retainers of both were present, on the 1st of January, 1630; when Rothiemay was killed, and several persons hurt on both sides. To stanch this bloody quarrel, the Marquis of Huntly, who was chief to both parties, and who had therefore a right to act as arbiter between them, ordered Frendraught to pay fifty thousand merks to Rothiemay's widow. In the ensuing September, Frendraught fell into another quarrel, in the course of which James Lesly, son to Lesly of Pitcaple, was shot through the arm. Soon after the last inci-

74-76. Ricklaw-holm is a place upon the Evan-water, which falls into the Annan, below Moffat. Wamphray-gate was in those days an alehouse.—S.

dent, Frendraught, having paid a visit to the Marquis of Huntly at the Bog of Gight, the Laird of Pitcaple came up with thirty armed men, to demand atonement for the wound of his son. Huntly acted in this case with great discretion. Without permitting the two lairds to come to a conference, he endeavored to persuade the complaining party that Frendraught was in reality innocent of his son's wound; and, as Pitcaple went away vowing vengeance, he sent Frendraught home under a strong escort, which was commanded by his son, the Viscount Aboyne, and by the young Laird of Rothiemay, son to him whom Frendraught had killed some months before. The party reached Frendraught Castle without being attacked by Pitcaple; when, Aboyne and Rothiemay offering to take leave of Frendraught and his lady, in order to return home, they were earnestly entreated by these individuals to remain a night, and postpone their return till to-morrow. Being with difficulty prevailed upon, the young Viscount and Rothiemay were well entertained, and after supper went cheerfully to bed. To continue the narrative in the words of Spalding—"The Viscount was laid in an bed in the Old Tower going off the hall, and standing upon a vault, wherein there was ane round hole, devised of old, just under Aboyne's bed. Robert Gordon, his servitor, and English Will, his page, were both laid in the same chamber. The Laird of Rothiemay, with some servants beside him, was laid in another chamber just above Aboyne's chamber; and in another room above that chamber, were laid George Chalmers of Noth, and George Gordon, another of the Viscount's servants; with them also was laid Captain Rolloch, then in Frendraught's own company. All being thus at rest, about midnight that dolorous tower took fire in so sudden and furious a manner, yea, and in ane clap, that the noble Viscount, the Laird of Rothiemay, English Will, Colonel Wat, another of Aboyne's servants, and other two, being six in number, were cruelly burnt and tormented to the death, without help or relief; the Laird of Frendraught, his lady, and haill household looking on, without moving or stirring to deliver them from the fury of this fearful fire, as was reported. Robert Gordon, called Sutherland Gordon, being in the Viscount's chamber, escaped this fire with the life. George Chalmers and Captain Rolloch, being in the third room, escaped this fire also, and, as was said, Aboyne might have saved himself also if he would have gone out of doors, which he would not do, but suddenly ran up stairs to Rothiemay's chamber, and wakened him to rise; and as he is awakening him, the timber passage and lofting of the chamber hastily takes fire, so that none of them could win down stairs again; so they turned to a window looking to the close, where they piteously cried many times, "Help! help! for God's cause!" The Laird and Lady, with their servants, all seeing and hearing the woeful crying, made no help or manner of helping; which they perceiving, cried oftentimes mercy at God's hands for their sins; syne clasped in each other's arms, and cheerfully suffered their martyrdom. Thus died this noble Viscount, of singular expectation, Rothiemay, a brave youth, and the rest, by this doleful fire, never enough to be deplored, to the great grief and sorrow of their kin, parents, and hail common people, especially to the noble Marquis, who for his good will got this reward. No man can express the dolour of him and his lady, nor yet the grief of the Viscount's own dear lady, when it came to her ears, which she kept to her dying day, disdaining after the company of men all her life-time, following the love of the turtle dove.

'It is reported that upon the morn after this woeful fire, the Lady Frendraught, daughter to the Earl of Sutherland, and near cousin to the Marquis, backed in a white plaid, and riding on a small nag, having a boy leading her horse, without any more in her company, in this pitiful manner she came weeping and mourning to the Bog, desiring entry to speak with my lord; but this was refused; so she returned back to her own house, the same gate she came, comfortless.' —SPALDING'S *History of the Troubles in Scotland.*

" Suspicion formed two theories regarding the cause of the fire of Frendraught. The first was, that the Laird had wilfully set fire to the tower, for the purpose of destroying the young Laird of Rothiemay. The other was, that it originated in the revengeful feelings of the Laird of Pitcaple. In the first theory there is extremely little probability. First, it could not have been premeditated; because the circumstance of Frendraught being accompanied home that day by Aboyne and Rothiemay, was entirely accidental. In the second place, there was no reason for Frendraught being inclined to murder Rothiemay, except that he grudged the payment of the fifty thousand merks to his mother; while there was every reason for his being inclined rather to befriend a youth whom he had already injured by occasioning the death of his father. In the third place, all Frendraught's family papers, with much gold and silver, both in money and plate, were consumed in the fire. And, in the fourth place, it is extremely improbable that any man of his rank should commit so deliberate and so atrocious an act of villainy. On the other hand, it seems by no means improbable that Pitcaple should have caused fire to be set to his enemy's house; a mode of reprisal which had been practised in the same district of country, as we have already seen, by a gentleman of only the preceding age. Pitcaple's men, moreover, had been heard to declare an intention of attempting some such enterprise against Frendraught; as was proved on the trial of a gentleman of the name of Meldrum, who was apprehended, condemned, and executed, for his alleged accession to their conspiracy."—CHAMBERS'S *Scottish Ballads*, p. 85.

This ballad was first printed in the *North Countrie Garland*, p. 4, and afterwards with a few slight corrections in Motherwell's *Minstrelsy*, having in both cases been furnished by Mr. C. K. Sharpe. The tragic story was celebrated by one Arthur Johnston, a contemporary scholar, in two Latin poems, the one entitled, *Querela Sophiæ Hay, dominæ de Melgeine, de morte mariti*, and the other, *De Johanne Gordonio, Vicecomite de Melgeine, el Johanne Gordonio de Rothemay, in arce Frendriaca combustis* (Finlay, i. 67). In Herd's Collection (i. 199) is a modern piece on the subject called *Frennet Hall*, in the detestable style of the last century. This very feeble production is also to be found in Ritson's *Scottish Songs* (ii. 31), Johnson's *Museum*, and elsewhere. But Ritson gives these few stanzas of an excellent old ballad, as remembered by the Rev. Mr. Boyd, the translator of Dante:

The reek it rose, and the flame it flew,
  And oh the fire augmented high,
Until it came to Lord John's chamber-window,
  And to the bed where Lord John lay.

"O help me, help me, Lady Frennet!
  I never ettled harm to thee;
And if my father slew my lord,
  Forget the deed and rescue me."

He looked east, he looked west,
  To see if any help was nigh;
At length his little page he saw,
  Who to his lord aloud did cry.

"Loup doun, loup doun, my master dear!
  What though the window's dreigh and hie?
I'll catch you in my arms twa,
  And never a foot from you I'll flee."

"How can I loup, you little page,
  How can I leave this window hie?
Do you not see the blazing low,
  And my twa legs burnt to my knee?"

THE eighteenth of October,
  A dismal tale to hear,
How good Lord John and Rothiemay
  Was both burnt in the fire.

When steeds was saddled and well bridled,
  And ready for to ride,
Then out it came her, false Frendraught,
  Inviting them to bide.

Said,—"Stay this night untill we sup,
  The morn untill we dine;
'Twill be a token of good 'greement
  'Twixt your good Lord and mine."

"We'll turn again," said good Lord John;—
  "But no," said Rothiemay,—
"My steed's trapan'd, my bridle's broken,
  I fear the day I'm fey."

When mass was sung, and bells was rung,
  And all men bound for bed,
Then good Lord John and Rothiemay
  In one chamber was laid.

They had not long cast off their cloaths,
  And were but now asleep,
When the weary smoke began to rise,
  Likewise the scorching heat.

"O waken, waken, Rothiemay!
  O waken, brother dear!
And turn you to our Saviour;
  There is strong treason here."

When they were dressed in their cloaths,
  And ready for to boun,
The doors and windows was all secur'd,
  The roof-tree burning down.

He did him to the wire-window,
As fast as he could gang;
Says,—"Wae to the hands put in the stancheons,
For out we'll never win."

When he stood at the wire-window,
Most doleful to be seen,
He did espy her, Lady Frendraught,
Who stood upon the green.

Cried,—"Mercy, mercy, Lady Frendraught!
Will ye not sink with sin?
For first your husband killed my father,
And now you burn his son."

O then out spoke her, Lady Frendraught,
And loudly did she cry,—
"It were great pity for good Lord John,
But none for Rothiemay.
But the keys are casten in the deep draw well,
Ye cannot get away."

While he stood in this dreadful plight,
Most piteous to be seen,
There called out his servant Gordon,
As he had frantic been.

"O loup, O loup, my dear master,
O loup and come to me!
I'll catch you in my arms two;
One foot I will not flee.

"O loup, O loup, my dear master,
O loup and come away!
I'll catch you in my arms two,
But Rothiemay may lie."

"The fish shall never swim in the flood,
Nor corn grow through the clay,
Nor the fiercest fire that ever was kindled
Twin me and Rothiemay.

"But I cannot loup, I cannot come,
I cannot win to thee;
My head's fast in the wire-window,
My feet burning from me.

"My eyes are seething in my head,
My flesh roasting also,
My bowels are boiling with my blood;
Is not that a woeful woe?

"Take here the rings from my white fingers
That are so long and small,
And give them to my lady fair,
Where she sits in her hall.

"So I cannot loup, I cannot come,
I cannot loup to thee;
My earthly part is all consumed,
My spirit but speaks to thee."

Wringing her hands, tearing her hair,
His lady she was seen,
And thus addressed his servant Gordon,
Where he stood on the green.

"O wae be to you, George Gordon,
An ill death may you die!
So safe and sound as you stand there,
And my lord bereaved from me."

"I bad him loup, I bad him come,
I bad him loup to me;
I'd catch him in my arms two,
A foot I should not flee. &c.

"He threw me the rings from his white fingers,
Which were so long and small,
To give to you, his lady fair,
Where you sat in your hall." &c.

Sophia Hay, Sophia Hay,
O bonny Sophia was her name,—
Her waiting maid put on her cloaths,
But I wot she tore them off again.

And aft she cried, "Ohon! alas, alas!
A sair heart's ill to win;
I wan a sair heart when I married him,
And the day it's well return'd again."

THE BONNIE HOUSE O' AIRLY.

Finlay's *Scottish Ballads*, ii. 31.

THE Earl of Airly, a nobleman zealously attached to the cause of King Charles, withdrew from Scotland in order to avoid subscribing the Covenant, leaving his eldest son Lord Ogilvie at home. The Committee of Estates, hearing that Airly had fled the country, directed the Earls of Montrose and Kinghorn to take possession of his castle, but in this, owing to the exceeding strength of the place, they did not succeed. Subsequently the Earl of Argyle, a personal enemy of the Earl of Airly, was charged with the same commission, and raised an army of five thousand men to carry out his trust. Lord Ogilvie was unable to hold out against such a force, and abandoned his father's stronghold, which, as well as his own residence of Forthar, was plundered and utterly destroyed by Argyle. Lady Ogilvie is said to have been pregnant at the time of the burning of Forthar, and to have undergone considerable danger before she could find proper refuge. She never had, however, more than one son, though she is endowed with no fewer than ten by the ballads. According to one account, the event here celebrated took place in 1639; another assigns it to 1640. (Napier's *Montrose and the Covenanters*, i. 533.)

The *Bonnie House of Airly* was first printed in Finlay's *Scottish Ballads*. Other copies are given in Cromek's *Remains of Nithsdale and Galloway Song*, p. 225; Smith's *Scottish Minstrel*, ii. 2; Hogg's *Jacobite*

Relics, ii. 152; Sharpe's *Ballad Book*, p. 59; and Kinloch's *Ancient Scottish Ballads*, p. 104.

A modern attempt on the same theme may be seen in Hogg's *Jacobite Relics*, ii. 411. Allan Cunningham, misled by the Ogilvies' continuing to the Pretender the devotion they exhibited to the Royal Martyr and his son, has transferred the burning of Airly to the 18th century. See his *Young Airly*, in Cromek's *Remains*, p. 196, and, rewritten, in *The Songs of Scotland*, iii. 218.

It fell on a day, and a bonnie summer day,
When the corn grew green and yellow,
That there fell out a great dispute
Between Argyle and Airly.

The Duke o' Montrose has written to Argyle
To come in the morning early,
An' lead in his men, by the back o' Dunkeld,
To plunder the bonnie house o' Airly.

The lady look'd o'er her window sae hie,
And O but she looked weary!
And there she espied the great Argyle
Come to plunder the bonnie house o' Airly.

"Come down, come down, Lady Margaret," he says,
"Come down and kiss me fairly,
Or before the morning clear daylight,
I'll no leave a standing stane in Airly."

"I wadna kiss thee, great Argyle,
I wadna kiss thee fairly,
I wadna kiss thee, great Argyle,
Gin you shoudna leave a standing stane in Airly."

He has ta'en her by the middle sae sma',
Says, "Lady, where is your drury?"
"It's up and down by the bonnie burn side,
Amang the planting of Airly."

They sought it up, they sought it down,
They sought it late and early,
And found it in the bonnie balm-tree,
That shines on the bowling-green o' Airly.

He has ta'en her by the left shoulder,
And O but she grat sairly,
And led her down to yon green bank,
Till he plundered the bonnie house o' Airly.

"O it's I hae seven braw sons," she says,
"And the youngest ne'er saw his daddie,
And altho' I had as mony mae,
I wad gie them a' to Charlie.

"But gin my good lord had been at hame,
As this night he is wi' Charlie,
There durst na a Campbell in a' the west
Hae plundered the bonnie house o' Airly."

THE BONNIE HOUSE OF AIRLY.

From Sharpe's *Ballad Book*, p. 59.

IT fell on a day, and a bonny simmer day,
  When green grew aits and barley,
That there fell out a greet dispute
  Between Argyll and Airlie.

Argyll has raised an hunder men,
  An hunder harness'd rarely,
And he's awa' by the back of Dunkell,
  To plunder the castle of Airlie.

Lady Ogilvie looks o'er her bower window,
  And O but she looks weary!
And there she spy'd the great Argyll,
  Come to plunder the bonny house of Airlie.

"Come down, come down, my Lady Ogilvie,
  Come down, and kiss me fairly:"
"O I winna kiss the fause Argyll,
  If he shouldna leave a standing stane in Airlie."

He hath taken her by the left shoulder,
  Says, "Dame where lies thy dowry?"
"O it's east and west yon water side,
  And it's down by the banks of the Airlie."

They hae sought it up, they hae sought it down,
  They have sought it maist severely,
Till they fand it in the fair plum-tree,
  That shines on the bowling-green of Airlie.

He hath taken her by the middle sae small,
  And O but she grat sairly!
And laid her down by the bonny burn-side,
  Till they plundered the castle of Airlie.

"Gif my gude lord war here this night,
  As he is with King Charlie,
Neither you, nor ony ither Scottish Lord,
  Durst awow to the plundering of Airlie.

"Gif my gude Lord war now at hame,
  As he is with his king,
Then durst nae a Campbell in a' Argyll
  Set fit on Airlie green.

"Ten bonny sons I have born unto him,
  The eleventh ne'er saw his daddy;
But though I had an hundred mair,
  I'd gie them a' to King Charlie.

THE BARON OF BRACKLEY.

First published as follows in Jamieson's *Popular Ballads*, i. 102. The copy used was derived from Mrs. Brown, and collated with a fragment taken down by Scott from the recitation of two of the descendants of Inverey. Buchan has given a different version in his *Gleanings*, which is annexed to the present. "This ballad," says Chambers, "records an unfortunate rencontre, which took place on the 16th of September, 1666, between John Gordon of Brackley, commonly called the Baron of Brackley, (in Aberdeenshire,) and Farquharson of Inverey, a noted freebooter, who dwelt on Dee-side. The former gentleman, who is yet remembered by tradition as a person of the most amiable and respectable character, had contrived to offend Farquharson, by pounding some horses belonging to his (Farquharson's) followers, which had either strayed into the Brackley grounds, or become forfeited on account of some petty delinquencies committed by their proprietors. Farquharson was a man of violent habits and passions; he is yet remembered by the epithet *Fuddie*, descriptive of his hurried, impatient gait; and it is said that, having been in league with the powers of darkness, he was buried on the north side of a hill, where the sun never shone. On account of the miraculous expedition with which he could sweep the cattle away from a fertile district, *Deil scoup wi'*

Fuddie! is still a popular proverb, implying that the devil could alone keep his own part with him. This singular marauder, it appears, from authentic information, wished at first to argue the point at issue with the Baron of Brackley; but in the course of the altercation some expression from one of the parties occasioned a mutual discharge of fire-arms, by which Brackley and three of his followers fell. An attempt was made by the baron's friends to bring Fuddie to justice; but the case seems to have been justly considered one of chance medley, and the accused party was soon restored to society.—*The Scottish Ballads*, p. 147.

DOWN Dee side came Inverey whistling and playing;
He's lighted at Brackley yates at the day dawing.

Says, "Baron o' Brackley, O are ye within?
There's sharp swords at the yate will gar your blood spin."

The lady raise up, to the window she went;
She heard her kye lowing o'er hill and o'er bent.

"O rise up, ye baron, and turn back your kye;
For the lads o' Drumwharran are driving them bye."

"How can I rise, lady, or turn them again!
Whare'er I have ae man, I wat they hae ten."

"Then rise up, my lasses, tak rocks in your hand,
And turn back the kye;—I ha'e you at command.

"Gin I had a husband, as I hae nane,
He wadna lye in his bower, see his kye ta'en."

Then up got the baron, and cried for his graith;
Says, "Lady, I'll gang, tho' to leave you I'm laith.

"Come, kiss me, then, Peggy, and gie me my speir;
I ay was for peace, tho' I never fear'd weir.

"Come, kiss me, then, Peggy, nor think I'm to blame;
I weel may gae out, but I'll never win in!"

When Brackley was busked, and rade o'er the closs,
A gallanter baron ne'er lap to a horse.

When Brackley was mounted, and rade o'er the green,
He was as bald a baron as ever was seen.

Tho' there cam' wi' Inverey thirty and three,
There was nane wi' bonny Brackley but his brother and he.

Twa gallanter Gordons did never sword draw;
But against four and thirty, wae's me, what is twa?

Wi' swords and wi' daggers they did him surround;
And they've pierced bonny Brackley wi' many a wound.

Frae the head o' the Dee to the banks o' the Spey,
The Gordons may mourn him, and bann Inverey.

"O came ye by Brackley yates, was ye in there?
Or saw ye his Peggy dear riving her hair?"

"O I came by Brackley yates, I was in there,
And I saw his Peggy a-making good cheer."

That lady she feasted them, carried them ben;
She laugh'd wi' the men that her baron had slain.

"O fye on you, lady! how could you do sae?
You open'd your yates to the fause Inverey."

She ate wi' him, drank wi' him, welcom'd him in;
She welcom'd the villain that slew her baron!

She kept him till morning, syne bade him be gane,
And shaw'd him the road that he shou'dna be taen.

"Thro' Birss and Aboyne," she says, "lyin in a tour,
O'er the hills o' Glentanar you'll skip in an hour."

—There's grief in the kitchen, and mirth in the ha';
But the Baron o' Brackley is dead and awa.

THE BARON OF BRAIKLEY.

Buchan's *Gleanings*, p. 68, taken from *Scarce Ancient Ballads*, p. 9.

INVEREY came down Deeside whistlin an playin,
He was at brave Braikley's yett ere it was dawin;
He rappit fou loudly, an wi a great roar,
Cried, "Cum down, cum down, Braikley, an open the door.

"Are ye sleepin, Baronne, or are ye wakin?
Ther's sharp swords at your yett will gar your bluid spin:
Open the yett, Braikley, an lat us within,
Till we on the green turf gar your bluid rin."

Out spak the brave Baronne owre the castell wa,
"Are ye come to spulzie an plunder my ha?
But gin ye be gentlemen, licht an cum in,
Gin ye drink o' my wine ye'll nae gar my bluid spin.

"Gin ye be hir'd widdifus, ye may gang by,
Ye may gang to the lawlands and steal their fat
ky;
Ther spulzie like revers o' wyld kettrin clan,
Wha plunder unsparing baith houses and lan'.

"Gin ye be gentlemen, licht an cum in,
Ther's meat an drink i' my ha' for every man:
Gin ye be hir'd widdifus, ye may gang by,
Gang down to the lawlans, an steal horse an
ky."

Up spak his ladie, at his bak where she laid,
"Get up, get up, Braikley, an be not afraid;
They're but hir'd widdifus wi belted plaids.
* * * * *

"Cum kis me, my Peggy, I'le nae langer stay,
For I will go out an meet Inverey;
But haud your tongue, Peggy, and mak nae sic
din,
For yon same hir'd widdifus will prove to be
men."

She called on her maries, they came to her han;
Cries, "Bring your rocks, lassies, we will them
coman;
Get up, get up, Braikley, and turn bak your ky,
For me an my women will them defy.

"Come forth than, my maidens, an show them some play;
We'll ficht them, an shortly the cowards will fly.
Gin I had a husband, wheras I hae nane,
He wadna ly in his bed and see his ky taen.

"Ther's four-an-twenty milk whit calves, twal o' them ky,
In the woods o' Glentanner it's ther they a' ly;
Ther are goats in the Etnach, an sheep o' the brae,
An a' will be plunderd by young Inverey."

"Now haud your tongue, Peggy, an gie me a gun,
Ye'll see me gae furth, but Ile never return.
Call my bruther William, my unkl also;
My cusin James Gordon, we'll mount an' we'll go."

Whan Braikley was ready an stood i the closs,
He was the bravest baronne that e'er munted horse;
Whan a' war assembld on the castell green,
Nae man like brave Braikley was ther to be seen.

"Turn back, bruther William, ye are a bride-groom,
* * * * *
We bonnie Jean Gordon, the maid o the mill,
O sichin and sobbin she'll seen get her fill."

"I'me nae coward, brither, it's kent I'me a man;
Ile ficht i' your quarral as lang's I can stan.
Ile ficht, my dear brither, wi heart an guid will,
An so will yung Harry that lives at the mill.

"But turn, my dear brither, and nae langer stay.
What'll cum o' your ladie, gin Braikley they slay?
What'll cum o' your ladie an' bonny yung son,
O what'll cum o' them when Braikley is gone?"

"I never will turn: do ye think I will fly?
No, here I will ficht, and here I will die."

"Strik dogs," cries Inverey, "an ficht till ye're slayn,
For we are four hunder, ye are but four men:
Strik, strik, ye proud boaster, your honor is gone,
Your lans we will plunder, your castell we'll burn."

At the head o' the Etnach the battel began,
At little Auchoilzie they killd the first man:
First they killd ane, an syne they killd twa,
They killd gallant Braikley, the flowr o' them a'.

They killd William Gordon and James o' the Knox,
An brave Alexander, the flowr o' Glenmuick:
What sichin an moaning war heard i the glen,
For the Baronne o' Braikley, wha basely was slayn!

"Came ye by the castell, an was ye in there?
Saw ye pretty Peggy tearing her hair?"
"Yes, I cam by Braikley, an I gaed in ther,
An ther saw his ladie braiding her hair.

"She was rantin, an' dancin, an' singin for joy,
An vowin that nicht she woud feest Inverey:
She eat wi him, drank wi him, welcomd him in,
Was kind to the man that had slayn her baronne."

Up spak the son on the nourices knee,
"Gin I live to be a man revenged Ile be."
Ther's dool i the kitchin, an mirth i the ha,
The Baronne o Braikley is dead an awa.

GILDEROY.

Gilderoy (properly Gilleroy) signifies in Gaelic "the red-haired lad." The person thus denoted was, according to tradition, one Patrick of the proscribed clan Gregor. The following account of him is taken from the *Scot's Musical Museum*, p. 71, vol. iv. ed. of 1853.

"Gilderoy was a notorious freebooter in the highlands of Perthshire, who, with his gang, for a considerable time infested the country, committing the most barbarous outrages on the inhabitants. Some of these

81. See *Johnie Armstrang*, p. 45.

ruffians, however, were at length apprehended through the vigilance and activity of the Stewarts of Athol, and conducted to Edinburgh, where they were tried, condemned, and executed, in February, 1638. Gilderoy, seeing his accomplices taken and hanged, went up, and in revenge burned several houses belonging to the Stewarts in Athol. This new act of atrocity was the prelude to his ruin. A proclamation was issued offering £1,000 for his apprehension. The inhabitants rose *en masse*, and pursued him from place to place, till at length he, with five more of his associates, was overtaken and secured. They were next carried to Edinburgh, where after trial and conviction, they expiated their offences on the gallows, in the month of July, 1638."

In the vulgar story-books, Gilderoy, besides committing various monstrous and unnatural crimes, enjoys the credit of having picked Cardinal Richelieu's pocket in the King's presence, robbed Oliver Cromwell, and hanged a judge.

The ballad *is said* to have been composed not long after the death of Gilderoy, " by a young woman of no mean talent, who unfortunately became attached to this daring robber, and had cohabited with him for some time before his being apprehended." A black-letter copy printed in England as early as 1650 has been preserved. Another, with " some slight variations," is contained " in Playford's *Wit and Mirth*, first edition of vol. iii., printed in 1703." The piece is next found in *Pills to purge Melancholy*, v. 39, and, with one different stanza, in *Old Ballads*, i. 271. In the second volume (p. 106) of Thomson's *Orpheus Caledonius* (1733), it appears with considerable alterations. Lady Elizabeth Wardlaw (*née* Halket) undertook a revision of the ballad, and by expunging two worthless stanzas and adding three (those enclosed in brackets), produced the version here given, which is taken from Ritson's *Scotish Songs*, ii. 24. Percy's copy (*Reliques*, i. 335) is the same, with the omission of the ninth stanza, and Herd and Pinkerton have followed Percy.

GILDEROY was a bonny boy,
Had roses tull his shoone ;
His stockings were of silken soy,
Wi' garters hanging doune.
It was, I weene, a comelie sight,
To see sae trim a boy ;
He was my jo and hearts delight,
My handsome Gilderoy.

O sik twa charming een he had,
A breath as sweet as rose ;
He never ware a Highland plaid,
But costly silken clothes.
He gain'd the luve of ladies gay,
Nane eir tul him was coy :
Ah, wae is me ! I mourn the day,
For my dear Gilderoy.

My Gilderoy and I were born
Baith in one toun together ;
We scant were seven years, beforn
We gan to luve each other ;

Our dadies and our mammies, thay
  Were fill'd wi' mickle joy,
To think upon the bridal day
  'Twixt me and Gilderoy.

For Gilderoy, that luve of mine,
  Gude faith, I freely bought
A wedding sark of holland fine,
  Wi' silken flowers wrought;
And he gied me a wedding ring,
  Which I receiv'd wi' joy;
Nae lad nor lassie eir could sing,
  Like me and Gilderoy.

Wi' mickle joy we spent our prime,
  Till we were baith sixteen,
And aft we passed the langsome time,
  Amang the leaves sae green;
Aft on the banks we'd sit us thair,
  And sweetly kiss and toy;
Wi' garlands gay wad deck my hair
  My handsome Gilderoy.

[O that he still had been content
  Wi' me to lead his life;
But ah, his manfu' heart was bent
  To stir in feates of strife:
And he in many a venturous deed
  His courage bauld wad try,

And now this gars mine heart to bleed
For my dear Gilderoy.

And whan of me his leave he tuik,
The tears they wat mine ee;
I gave tull him a parting luik,
"My benison gang wi' thee!
God speid thee weil, mine ain dear heart,
For gane is all my joy;
My heart is rent sith we maun part,
My handsome Gilderoy."]

My Gilderoy, baith far and near,
Was fear'd in every toun,
And bauldly bare away the gear
Of many a lawland loun.
Nane eir durst meet him man to man,
He was sae brave a boy;
At length wi' numbers he was tane,
My winsome Gilderoy.

[The Queen of Scots possessed nought
That my love let me want,
For cow and ew he 'to me brought,'
And een whan they were skant.
All these did honestly possess
He never did annoy,
Who never fail'd to pay their cess
To my love Gilderoy.]

Wae worth the loun that made the laws,
To hang a man for gear;
To reave of live for ox or ass,
For sheep, or horse, or mare!
Had not their laws been made sae strick,
I neir had lost my joy,
Wi' sorrow neir had wat my cheek
For my dear Gilderoy.

Giff Gilderoy had done amisse,
He mought hae banisht been;
Ah! what sair cruelty is this,
To hang sike handsome men!
To hang the flower o' Scottish land,
Sae sweet and fair a boy!
Nae lady had sae white a hand
As thee, my Gilderoy.

Of Gilderoy sae fraid they were,
They bound him mickle strong;
Tull Edenburrow they led him thair,
And on a gallows hung:
They hung him high aboon the rest,
He was sae trim a boy;
Thair dyed the youth whom I lued best,
My handsome Gilderoy.

Thus having yielded up his breath,
I bare his corpse away;

Wi' tears that trickled for his death
I washt his comelye clay ;
And siker in a grave sae deep,
I laid the dear-loed boy,
And now for evir maun I weep
My winsome Gilderoy.

ROB ROY.

THE subject of this piece is the abduction of a young Scottish lady by a son of the celebrated Rob Roy Macgregor. Sentence of outlawry had been pronounced against this person for not appearing to stand his trial for murder. While under this sentence, he conceived the desperate project of carrying off Jane Kay, heiress of Edinbelly, in Sterlingshire, and obtaining possession of her estate by a forced marriage. Engaging a party of the proscribed Macgregors to assist him in this enterprise, Rob Roy entered the young woman's house with his brother James, tied her, hand and foot, with ropes, and carried her thus on horseback to the abode of one of his clan in Argyleshire, where, after some mock ceremony, she was compelled to submit to his embraces. The place in which the unfortunate woman was detained, was discovered, and she was rescued by her family. Rob Roy and James Macgregor were tried for their lives. The latter escaped from prison, but the principal in this outrage suffered condign punishment in February, 1753.

Fragments of the story were printed in *Select Scotish Songs*, by Robert Burns, edited by R. H. Cromek, ii. 199, and in Maidment's *North Countrie Garland*, p. 44; a complete copy in the *Thistle of Scotland*, p. 93. Chambers has combined the fragments of Burns and Maidment with a third version furnished by Mr. Kinloch, and has produced a ballad which is on the whole the most eligible for this place. (*Scottish Ballads*, p. 175.) In the Appendix may be seen the editions above referred to, and also *Eppie Morrie*, a ballad founded on a similar incident.

This sort of kidnapping seems to have been the commonest occurrence in the world in Scotland. Sharpe has collected not a few cases in his *Ballad Book*, p. 99, and he gives us two stanzas of another ballad.

The Highlandmen hae a' cum down,
They've a' come down almost,
They've stowen away the bonny lass,
The Lady of Arngosk.

Behind her back they've tied her hands,
An' then they set her on;
"I winna gang wi' you," she said,
"Nor ony Highland loon."

Rob Roy frae the Hielands cam
Unto the Lawland Border,
To steal awa a gay ladye,
To haud his house in order.

He cam ower the loch o' Lynn,
Twenty men his arms did carry;

Himsell gaed in and fand her out,
  Protesting he would marry.

When he cam he surrounded the house,
  No tidings there cam before him,
Or else the lady would have gone,
  For still she did abhor him.

" O will ye gae wi' me ? " he says,
  " O will ye be my honey ?
O will ye be my wedded wife ?
  For I loe ye best of ony."

" I winna gae wi' you," she says,
  " I winna be your honey ;
I winna be your wedded wife,
  Ye loe me for my money."

* * * * *

Wi' mournful cries and watery eyes,
  Fast hauding by her mother,
Wi' mournful cries and watery eyes,
  They were parted frae each other.

He gied her nae time to be dress'd,
  As ladies do when they're brides,
But he hastened and hurried her awa,
  And rowed her in his plaids.

He mounted her upon a horse,
  Himsell lap on behind her,

And they're awa to the Hieland hills,
  Where her friends may never find her.

As they gaed ower the Hieland hills,
  The lady aften fainted,
Saying, "Wae be to my cursed gowd,
  This road to me invented!"

They rade till they came to Ballyshine,
  At Ballyshine they tarried;
He brought to her a cotton gown,
  Yet ne'er wad she be married.

Two held her up before the priest,
  Four carried her to bed O;
Maist mournfully she wept and cried,
  When she by him was laid O!

[*The tune changes.*]

"O be content, O be content,
  O be content to stay, lady,
For now ye are my wedded wife
  Until my dying day, lady.

"Rob Roy was my father call'd,
  Macgregor was his name, lady;
He led a band o' heroes bauld,
  And I am here the same, lady.

"He was a hedge unto his friends,
  A heckle to his foes, lady,
And every one that did him wrang,
  He took him by the nose, lady.

"I am as bold, I am as bold
  As my father was afore, lady;
He that daurs dispute my word
  Shall feel my gude claymore, lady.

"My father left me cows and yowes,
  And sheep, and goats, and a', lady,
And you and twenty thousand merks
  Will mak me a man fu' braw, lady."

BOOK VII.

QUEEN ELEANOR'S CONFESSION.

ELEANOR of Aquitaine was divorced from her first husband, Louis VII. of France, on account of misbehavior at Antioch, during the Second Crusade. Her conduct after her second marriage, with Henry II. of England, is agreed to have been irreproachable on the score of chastity. It is rather hard, therefore, that her reputation should be assailed as it is here; but if we complain of this injustice, what shall we say when we find, further on, the same story, with others even more ridiculous, told of the virtuous Eleanor of Castile, wife of Edward I.? See Peele's *Chronicle History of Edward I.*, Dyce's ed. i. 185, 188, *seq.*, and the ballad in vol. vii., 291. Both of these ballads are indeed pretty specimens of the historical value of popular traditions. The idea of the unlucky shrift is borrowed from some old story-teller. It occurs in the *fabliau Du Chevalier qui fist sa Fame confesse*, Barbazan, ed. Méon, iii. 229, in Boccaccio G. vii. 5, Bandello, Malespini, &c.; also in La Fontaine's *Le Mari Confesseur.*

The following ballad is from the *Collection* of 1723, vol. i. p. 18. There are several other versions: Percy's *Reliques*, ii. 165 (with corrections); Buchan's *Gleanings*, p. 77; Motherwell's *Minstrelsy*, p. 1 (*Earl Marshal*, from recitation); Aytoun's *Ballads of Scotland*, new ed. i. 196; Kinloch's *Ancient Scottish Ballads*, p. 247.

Queen Eleanor was a sick woman,
And afraid that she should dye;
Then she sent for two fryars of France,
To speak with her speedily.

The King call'd down his nobles all,
By one, by two, by three,
And sent away for Earl Marshal,
To speak with him speedily.

When that he came before the King,
He fell on his bended knee;
"A boon, a boon, our gracious king,
That you sent so hastily."

"I'll pawn my lands," the King then cry'd,
"My sceptre and my crown,
That whatsoe're Queen Eleanor says,
I will not write it down.

"Do you put on a fryar's coat,
And I'll put on another;
And we will to Queen Eleanor go,
Like fryar and his brother."

Thus both attired then they go:
When they came to Whitehall,
The bells did ring, and the choristers sing,
And the torches did light them all.

When that they came before the Queen,
  They fell on their bended knee;
"A boon, a boon, our gracious queen,
  That you sent so hastily."

"Are you two fryars of France," she said,
  "As I suppose you be?
But if you are two English fryars,
  Then hanged you shall be."

"We are two fryars of France," they said,
  "As you suppose we be;
We have not been at any mass
  Since we came from the sea."

"The first vile thing that e're I did,
  I will to you unfold;
Earl Marshal had my maidenhead,
  Beneath this cloth of gold."

"That's a vile sin," then said the King;
  "God may forgive it thee!"
"Amen, amen!" quoth Earl Marshal;
  With a heavy heart spoke he.

"The next vile thing that e're I did,
  To you I'll not deny;
I made a box of poyson strong,
  To poyson King Henry."

"That's a vile sin," then said the King,
  "God may forgive it thee!"
"Amen, amen!" quoth Earl Marshal;
  "And I wish it so may be."

"The next vile thing that e're I did,
  To you I will discover;
I poysoned fair Rosamond,
  All in fair Woodstock bow'r."

"That's a vile sin," then said the King;
  "God may forgive it thee!"
"Amen, amen!" quoth Earl Marshal;
  "And I wish it so may be."

"Do you see yonder's [a] little boy,
  A tossing of the ball?
That is Earl Marshal's eldest son,
  I love him the best of all.

"Do you see yonder's [a] little boy,
  A catching of the ball?
That is King Henry's son," she said;
  "I love him the worst of all.

"His head is like unto a bull,
  His nose is like a boar,"—
"No matter for that," King Henry cry'd,
  "I love him the better therefore."

The king pull'd off his fryar's coat,
And appeared all in red;
She shriek'd, she cry'd, and wrung her hands,
And said she was betray'd.

The King look'd over his left shoulder,
And a grim look looked he;
And said, "Earl Marshal, but for my oath,
Or hanged shouldst thou be."

From Kinloch's *Ancient Scottish Ballads*, 247.

THE Queen fell sick, and very, very sick,
She was sick, and like to dee,
And she sent for a friar oure frae France,
Her cónfessour to be.

King Henry, when he heard o' that,
An angry man was he;
And he sent to the Earl Marshall,
Attendance for to gie.

"The Queen is sick," King Henry cried,
"And wants to be beshriven;
She has sent for a friar oure frae France;
By the rude, he were better in heaven!

" But tak you now a friar's guise,
  The voice and gesture feign,
And when she has the pardon crav'd,
  Respond to her, Amen!

"And I will be a prelate old,
  And sit in a corner dark,
To hear the adventures of my spouse,
  My spouse, and her holy spark."

" My liege, my liege, how can I betray
  My mistress and my queen!
O swear by the rude, that no damage
  From this shall be gotten or gien!"

" I swear by the rude," quoth King Henry,
  " No damage shall be gotten or gien,
Come, let us spare no cure nor care
  For the conscience o' the Queen."

* * * * *

" O fathers, O fathers, I'm very, very sick,
  I'm sick, and like to dee;
Some ghostly comfort to my poor soul
  O tell if ye can gie!"

" Confess, confess," Earl Marshall cried,
  "And ye shall pardoned be:
" Confess, confess," the King replied,
  "And we shall comfort gie."

"O how shall I tell the sorry, sorry tale!
  How can the tale be told!
I play'd the harlot wi' the Earl Marshall
  Beneath yon cloth of gold.

"O wasna that a sin, and a very great sin!
  But I hope it will pardoned be:"
"Amen! Amen!" quoth the Earl Marshall,
  And a very fear't heart had he.

"O down i' the forest, in a bower,
  Beyond yon dark oak tree,
I drew a penknife frae my pocket
  To kill King Henerie.

"O wasna that a sin, and a very great sin!
  But I hope it will pardoned be:"
"Amen! Amen!" quoth the Earl Marshall,
  And a very fear't heart had he.

"O do you see yon pretty little boy,
  That's playing at the ba'?
He is the Earl Marshall's only son,
  And I loved him best of a'.

"O wasna that a sin, and a very great sin!
  But I hope it will pardoned be:"
"Amen! Amen!" quoth the Earl Marshall,
  And a very fear't heart had he.

"And do you see yon pretty little girl,
That's a' beclad in green?
She's a friar's daughter, oure in France,
And I hoped to see her a queen.

" O wasna that a sin, and a very great sin!
But I hope it will pardoned be:"
"Amen! Amen!" quoth the Earl Marshall,
And a fear't heart still had he.

" O do you see yon other little boy,
That's playing at the ba'?
He is King Henry's only son,
And I like him warst of a'.

" He's headed like a buck," she said,
"And backed like a bear,"—
"Amen!" quoth the King, in the King's ain voice,
" He shall be my only heir."

The King look'd over his left shoulder,
An angry man was he:
"An it werna for the oath I sware,
Earl Marshall, thou shouldst dee."

AULD MAITLAND.

From *Minstrelsy of the Scottish Border*, i. 306.

"THIS ballad, notwithstanding its present appearance, has a claim to very high antiquity. It has been preserved by tradition; and is, perhaps, the most authentic instance of a long and very old poem, exclusively thus preserved. It is only known to a few old people upon the sequestered banks of the Ettrick, and is published, as written down from the recitation of the mother of Mr. James Hogg, who sings, or rather chants it, with great animation. She learned the ballad from a blind man, who died at the advanced age of ninety, and is said to have been possessed of much traditionary knowledge. Although the language of this poem is much modernized, yet many words, which the reciters have retained without understanding them, still preserve traces of its antiquity. Such are the words *springals* (corruptedly pronounced *springwalls*), *sowies*, *portcullize*, and many other appropriate terms of war and chivalry, which could never have been introduced by a modern ballad-maker[?]. The incidents are striking and well managed; and they are in strict conformity with the manners of the age in which they are placed.

"The date of the ballad cannot be ascertained with any degree of accuracy. Sir Richard Maitland, the hero of the poem, seems to have been in possession of his estate about 1250; so that, as he survived the commencement of the wars betwixt England and Scotland, in 1296, his prowess against the English, in defence of his castle of Lauder or Thirlestane, must have been exerted during his extreme old age.

"The castle of Thirlestane is situated upon the Leader, near the town of Lauder. Whether the present building, which was erected by Chancellor Maitland, and improved by the duke of Lauderdale, occupies the site of the ancient castle, I do not know; but it still merits the epithet of a "*darksome house.*" I find no notice of the siege in history; but there is nothing improbable in supposing, that the castle, during the stormy period of the Baliol wars, may have held out against the English. The creation of a nephew of Edward I., for the pleasure of slaying him by the hand of young Maitland, is a poetical license; * and may induce us to place the date of the composition about the reign of David II., or of his successor, when the real exploits of Maitland and his sons were in some degree obscured, as well as magnified, by the lapse of time. The inveterate hatred against the English, founded upon the usurpation of Edward I., glows in every line of the ballad.

"Auld Maitland is placed, by Gawain Douglas, Bishop of Dunkeld, among the popular heroes of romance, in his allegorical Palice of Honour.

* Such liberties with the genealogy of monarchs were common to romancers. Henry the Minstrel makes Wallace slay more than one of King Edward's nephews; and Johnie Armstrong claims the merit of slaying a sister's son of Henry VIII. — S. (See p. 49.)

"I saw Raf Coilyear with his thrawin brow,
Crabit John the Reif, and auld Cowkilbeis Sow;
And how the wran cam out of Ailesay,
And Piers Plowman, that meid his workmen fow:
Gret Gowmacmorne, and Fin Mac Cowl, and how
They suld be goddis in Ireland, as they say.
Thair saw I Maitland upon auld beird gray,
Robin Hude, and Gilbert with the quhite hand,
How Hay of Nauchton flew in Madin land."

"It is a curious circumstance that this interesting tale, so often referred to by ancient authors, should be now recovered in so perfect a state; and many readers may be pleased to see the following sensible observations, made by a person born in Ettrick Forest, in the humble situation of a shepherd: 'I am surprised to hear that this song is suspected by some to be a modern forgery; the contrary will be best proved, by most of the old people, hereabouts, having a great part of it by heart. Many, indeed, are not aware of the manners of this country; till this present age, the poor illiterate people, in these glens, knew of no other entertainment, in the long winter nights, than repeating, and listening to, the feats of their ancestors, recorded in songs, which I believe to be handed down, from father to son, for many generations, although, no doubt, had a copy been taken, at the end of every fifty years, there must have been some difference, occasioned by the gradual change of language. I believe it is thus that many very ancient songs have been gradually modernized, to the common ear; while, to the connoisseur, they present marks of their genuine antiquity.'—*Letter to the Editor, from* Mr. James Hogg. [June 30, 1801.] To the observations of my ingenious correspondent I have nothing to add, but that, in this, and a thousand other instances, they accurately coincide with my personal knowledge."—SCOTT.

Notwithstanding the authority of Scott and Leyden, I am inclined to agree with Mr. Aytoun, (*Ballads of Scotland*, ii. 1,) that this ballad is a modern imitation, or if not that, a comparatively recent composition. It is with reluctance that I make for it the room it requires.

THERE lived a king in southern land,
King Edward hight his name;
Unwordily he wore the crown,
Till fifty years were gane.

He had a sister's son o's ain,
Was large of blood and bane;
And afterward, when he came up,
Young Edward hight his name.

One day he came before the king,
And kneel'd low on his knee—
"A boon, a boon, my good uncle,
I crave to ask of thee!

"At our lang wars, in fair Scotland,
I fain hae wish'd to be;
If fifteen hundred waled wight men
You'll grant to ride wi' me."

"Thou sall hae thae, thou sall hae mae;
I say it sickerlie;

And I mysell, an auld gray man,
  Array'd your host sall see."

King Edward rade, King Edward ran—
  I wish him dool and pyne!
Till he had fifteen hundred men
  Assembled on the Tyne.

And thrice as many at Berwicke
  Were all for battle bound,
[Who, marching forth with false Dunbar,
  A ready welcome found.]

They lighted on the banks of Tweed,
  And blew their coals sae het,
And fired the Merse and Teviotdale,
  All in an evening late.

As they fared up o'er Lammermore,
  They burn'd baith up and down,
Until they came to a darksome house,
  Some call it Leader-Town.

"Wha hauds this house?" young Edward cry'd,
  "Or wha gies't ower to me?"

25. North-Berwick, according to some reciters.—S.

27, 28. These two lines have been inserted by Mr. Hogg, to complete the verse. Dunbar, the fortress of Patrick, Earl of March, was too often opened to the English, by the treachery of that baron, during the reign of Edward I.—S.

A gray-hair'd knight set up his head,
And crackit richt crousely:

"Of Scotland's king I haud my house;
He pays me meat and fee;
And I will keep my guid auld house,
While my house will keep me."

They laid their sowies to the wall,
Wi' mony a heavy peal;
But he threw ower to them agen
Baith pitch and tar barrel.

With springalds, stanes, and gads of airn,
Amang them fast he threw;
Till mony of the Englishmen
About the wall he slew.

Full fifteen days that braid host lay,
Sieging Auld Maitland keen;
Syne they hae left him, hail and feir,
Within his strength of stane.

Then fifteen barks, all gaily good,
Met them upon a day,
Which they did lade with as much spoil
As they could bear away.

"England's our ain by heritage;
And what can us withstand,

Now we hae conquer'd fair Scotland,
  With buckler, bow, and brand?"

Then they are on to the land o' France,
  Where auld King Edward lay,
Burning baith castle, tower, and town,
  That he met in his way.

Until he came unto that town,
  Which some call Billop-Grace;
There were Auld Maitland's sons, a' three,
  Learning at school, alas!

The eldest to the youngest said,
  "O see ye what I see?
Gin a' be trew yon standard says,
  We're fatherless a' three.

"For Scotland's conquer'd up and down;
  Landmen we'll never be:
Now, will you go, my brethren two,
  And try some jeopardy?"

70. If this be a Flemish or Scottish corruption for Ville de Grace, in Normandy, that town was never besieged by Edward I., whose wars in France were confined to the province of Gascony. The rapid change of scene, from Scotland to France, excites a suspicion that some verses may have been lost in this place.—S.

75. Edward had quartered the arms of Scotland with his own.—S.

Then they hae saddled twa black horse,
  Twa black horse and a gray;
And they are on to King Edward's host,
  Before the dawn of day.

When they arrived before the host,
  They hover'd on the lay—
"Wilt thou lend me our king's standard,
  To bear a little way?"

"Where wast thou bred? where wast thou born?
  Where, or in what countrie?"
"In north of England I was born:"
  (It needed him to lie.)

"A knight me gat, a lady bore,
  I am a squire of high renowne;
I well may bear't to any king,
  That ever yet wore crowne."

"He ne'er came of an Englishman,
  Had sic an ee or bree;
But thou art the likest Auld Maitland,
  That ever I did see.

"But sic a gloom on ae browhead,
  Grant I ne'er see again!
For mony of our men he slew,
  And mony put to pain."

When Maitland heard his father's name,
An angry man was he!
Then, lifting up a gilt dagger,
Hung low down by his knee,

He stabb'd the knight the standard bore,
He stabb'd him cruellie;
Then caught the standard by the neuk,
And fast away rode he.

"Now, is't na time, brothers," he cried,
"Now, is't na time to flee?"
"Ay, by my sooth!" they baith replied,
"We'll bear you company."

The youngest turn'd him in a path,
And drew a burnish'd brand,
And fifteen of the foremost slew,
Till back the lave did stand.

He spurr'd the gray into the path,
Till baith his sides they bled—
"Gray! thou maun carry me away,
Or my life lies in wad!"

The captain lookit ower the wa',
About the break o' day;
There he beheld the three Scots lads,
Pursued along the way.

"Pull up portcullize! down draw-brigg!
My nephews are at hand;
And they sall lodge wi' me to-night,
In spite of all England."

Whene'er they came within the yate,
They thrust their horse them frae,
And took three lang spears in their hands,
Saying, "Here sall come nae mae!"

And they shot out, and they shot in,
Till it was fairly day;
When mony of the Englishmen
About the draw-brigg lay.

Then they hae yoked carts and wains,
To ca' their dead away,
And shot auld dykes abune the lave,
In gutters where they lay.

The king, at his pavilion door,
Was heard aloud to say,
"Last night, three o' the lads o' France
My standard stole away.

"Wi' a fause tale, disguised, they came,
And wi' a fauser trayne;
And to regain my gaye standard,
These men were a' down slayne."

"It ill befits," the youngest said,
"A crowned king to lie;
But, or that I taste meat and drink,
Reproved sall he be."

He went before King Edward straight,
And kneel'd low on his knee;
"I wad hae leave, my lord," he said,
"To speak a word wi' thee."

The king he turn'd him round about,
And wistna what to say—
Quo' he, "Man, thou's hae leave to speak,
Though thou should speak a' day."

"Ye said that three young lads o' France
Your standard stole away,
Wi' a fause tale, and a fauser trayne,
And mony men did slay.

"But we are nane the lads o' France,
Nor e'er pretend to be;
We are three lads o' fair Scotland,
Auld Maitland's sons are we;

"Nor is there men, in a' your host,
Daur fight us three to three."
"Now, by my sooth," young Edward said,
"Weel fitted ye sall be!

"Piercy sall with the eldest fight,
And Ethert Lunn wi' thee:
William of Lancaster the third,
And bring your fourth to me!"

[" Remember, Piercy, aft the Scot
Has cower'd beneath thy hand:]
For every drap of Maitland blood,
I'll gie a rig of land."

He clanked Piercy ower the head,
A deep wound and a sair,
Till the best blood o' his bodie
Came rinning down his hair.

"Now, I've slayne ane; slay ye the twa;
And that's gude companye;
And if the twa suld slay ye baith,
Ye'se get na help frae me."

But Ethert Lunn, a baited bear,
Had many battles seen;
He set the youngest wonder sair,
Till the eldest he grew keen.

"I am nae king, nor nae sic thing:
My word it shanna stand!
For Ethert sall a buffet bide,
Come he beneath my brand."

181, 182, supplied by Hogg.

He clankit Ethert ower the head,
 A deep wound and a sair,
Till the best blood of his bodie
 Came rinning ower his hair.

"Now I've slayne twa; slaye ye the ane;
 Isna that gude companye?
And tho' the ane suld slaye ye baith,
 Ye'se get nae help o' me."

The twa-some they hae slayne the ane;
 They maul'd him cruellie;
Then hung them over the draw-brigg,
 That all the host might see.

They rade their horse, they ran their horse,
 Then hover'd on the lee:
"We be three lads o' fair Scotland,
 That fain would fighting see."

This boasting when young Edward heard,
 An angry man was he:
"I'll tak yon lad, I'll bind yon lad,
 And bring him bound to thee!"

"Now God forbid," King Edward said,
 "That ever thou suld try!
Three worthy leaders we hae lost,
 And thou the fourth wad lie.

"If thou shouldst hang on yon draw-brigg,
Blythe wad I never be:"
But, wi' the poll-axe in his hand,
Upon the brigg sprang he.

The first stroke that young Edward gae,
He struck wi' might and mayn;
He clove the Maitland's helmet stout,
And bit right nigh the brayn.

When Maitland saw his ain blood fa',
An angry man was he:
He let his weapon frae him fa',
And at his throat did flee.

And thrice about he did him swing,
Till on the grund he light,
Where he has halden young Edward,
Tho' he was great in might.

"Now let him up," King Edward cried,
"And let him come to me:
And for the deed that thou hast done,
Thou shalt hae erldomes three."

"It's ne'er be said in France, nor e'er
In Scotland, when I'm hame,
That Edward once lay under me,
And e'er gat up again!"

247. Some reciters repeat it thus:—

He pierced him through and through the heart,
He maul'd him cruellie;
Then hung him ower the draw-brigg,
Beside the other three.

"Now take frae me that feather-bed,
Make me a bed o' strae!
I wish I hadna lived this day,
To mak my heart sae wae.

"If I were ance at London Tower,
Where I was wont to be,
I never mair suld gang frae hame,
Till borne on a bier-tree."

WILLIE WALLACE.

AFTER the battle of Roslin, we are informed by Bower, the continuator of Fordun's *Scotichronicon*, Wallace took ship for France, and various songs, both in that kingdom and in Scotland, he goes on to say, bear witness to the courage with which he encountered the attacks of pirates on the ocean, and of the English on the continent. Whatever we may think

"That *Englishman* lay under me,"
which is in the true spirit of Blind Harry, who makes Wallace say,
"I better like to see the Southeron die,
Than gold or land, that they can gie to me."—S.

of Wallace's expedition to France, there can be no doubt that the hero's exploits were at an early date celebrated in popular song. Still, the ballads which are preserved relate to only one of Wallace's adventures, and are of doubtful antiquity.

Burns communicated to Johnson's *Museum* (p. 498) a defective ballad called *Gude Wallace*. A better copy of this, from tradition, is here given. It is taken from Buchan's *Gleanings* (p. 114), and was derived by the editor from a wandering gipsy tinker. Mr. Laing has inserted in the notes to the new edition of Johnson's *Museum* (iv. 458*) what may perhaps be the original of both these recited ballads, though inferior to either. This copy appeared in a chap-book with some Jacobite ballads, about the year 1750. There are two other versions of this same story, in which Wallace's mistress is induced to betray him to the English, but repents in time to save her lover. The best of these is annexed to the present ballad. The other, which is but a fragment, is printed in Buchan's larger collection, ii. 226, *Wallace and his Leman*.

The principal incidents of this story are to be found in the Fifth Book of Blind Harry's Metrical *Life of Wallace*.

Jamieson, in *Popular Ballads*, ii. 166, and Cunningham, in *The Songs of Scotland*, i. 262, have taken the stanzas in Johnson's *Museum* as the basis of ballads of their own.

Wallace in the high highlans,
  Neither meat nor drink got he ;
Said, " Fa' me life, or fa' me death,
  Now to some town I maun be."

He's put on his short claiding,
And on his short claiding put he;
Says, "Fa' me life, or fa' me death,
Now to Perth-town I maun be."

He stepped o'er the river Tay,
I wat he stepped on dry land;
He wasna aware of a well-fared maid
Was washing there her lilie hands.

"What news, what news, ye well-fared maid?
What news hae ye this day to me?"
"No news, no news, ye gentle knight,
No news hae I this day to thee,
But fifteen lords in the hostage house
Waiting Wallace for to see."

"If I had but in my pocket
The worth of one single pennie,
I would go to the hostage house,
And there the gentlemen to see."

She put her hand in her pocket,
And she has pull'd out half-a-crown;
Says, "Take ye that, ye belted knight,
'Twill pay your way till ye come down."

As he went from the well-fared maid,
A beggar bold I wat met he,

Was cover'd wi' a clouted cloak,
And in his hand a trusty tree.

"What news, what news, ye silly auld man?
What news hae ye this day to gie?"
"No news, no news, ye belted knight,
No news hae I this day to thee,
But fifteen lords in the hostage house
Waiting Wallace for to see."

"Ye'll lend me your clouted cloak,
That covers you frae head to shie,
And I'll go to the hostage house,
Asking there for some supplie."

Now he's gone to the West-muir wood,
And there he's pull'd a trusty tree;
And then he's on to the hostage gone,
Asking there for charitie.

Down the stair the captain comes,
Aye the poor man for to see:
"If ye be a captain as good as ye look,
Ye'll give a poor man some supplie;
If ye be a captain as good as ye look,
A guinea this day ye'll gie to me."

"Where were ye born, ye crooked carle?
Where were ye born, in what countrie?"

"In fair Scotland I was born,
  Crooked carle that I be."

"I would give you fifty pounds,
  Of gold and white monie,
I would give you fifty pounds,
  If the traitor Wallace ye'd let me see."

"Tell down your money," said Willie Wallace,
  "Tell down your money, if it be good;
I'm sure I have it in my power,
  And never had a better bode.

"Tell down your money, if it be good,
  And let me see if it be fine;
I'm sure I have it in my power
  To bring the traitor Wallace in."

The money was told on the table,
  Silver bright of pounds fiftie:
"Now here I stand," said Willie Wallace,
  "And what hae ye to say to me?"

He slew the captain where he stood,
  The rest they did quack an' roar;
He slew the rest around the room,
  And ask'd if there were any more.

"Come, cover the table," said Willie Wallace,
  "Come, cover the table now, make haste;

For it will soon be three lang days
Sin I a bit o' meat did taste."

The table was not well covered,
Nor yet was he set down to dine,
Till fifteen more of the English lords
Surrounded the house where he was in.

The guidwife she ran but the floor,
And aye the guidman he ran ben;
From eight o'clock till four at noon
He had kill'd full thirty men.

He put the house in sic a swither
That five o' them he sticket dead,
Five o' them he drown'd in the river,
And five hung in the West-muir wood.

Now he is on to the North-Inch gone,
Where the maid was washing tenderlie;
"Now by my sooth," said Willie Wallace,
"It's been a sair day's wark to me."

He's put his hand in his pocket,
And he has pull'd out twenty pounds;
Says, "Take ye that, ye weel-fared maid
For the gude luck of your half-crown."

91. A beautiful plain, or common, lying along the Tay near Perth.—CHAMBERS.

SIR WILLIAM WALLACE.

From *The Thistle of Scotland*, p. 100.

THE editor states that he took the ballad down from the recitation of an old gentlewoman in Aberdeenshire.

WOU'D ye hear of William Wallace,
An' sek him as he goes,
Into the lan' of Lanark,
Amang his mortel faes?

There was fyften English sogers
Unto his ladie cam,
Said "Gie us William Wallace,
That we may have him slain.

"Wou'd ye gie William Wallace,
That we may have him slain,
And ye's be wedded to a lord,
The best in Christendeem."

"This verra nicht at seven,
Brave Wallace will come in,
And he'll come to my chamber door,
Without or dread or din."

The fyften English sogers
Around the house did wait,

And four brave Southron foragers,
  Stood hie upon the gait.

That verra nicht at seven
  Brave Wallace he came in,
And he came to his ladies bouir,
  Withouten dread or din.

When she beheld him Wallace,
  She star'd him in the face;
"Ohon, alas!" said that ladie,
  "This is a woful case.

"For I this nicht have sold you,
  This nicht you must be taen,
And I'm to be wedded to a lord,
  The best in Christendeem."

"Do you repent," said Wallace,
  "The ill you've dane to me?"
"Ay, that I do," said that ladie,
  "And will do till I die.

"Ay, that I do," said that ladie,
  "And will do ever still,
And for the ill I've dane to you,
  Let me burn upon a hill."

"Now God forfend," says brave Wallace,
  "I shou'd be so unkind;
Whatever I am to Scotland's faes,
  I'm aye a woman's friend.

"Will ye gie me your gown, your gown,
Your gown but and your kirtle,
Your petticoat of bonny brown,
And belt about my middle?

"I'll take a pitcher in ilka hand,
And do me to the well,
They'll think I'm one of your maidens,
Or think it is your sell."

She has gien him her gown, her gown,
Her petticoat and kirtle,
Her broadest belt wi' silver clasp,
To bind about his middle.

He's taen a pitcher in ilka hand,
And dane him to the well,
They thought him one of her maidens,
They ken'd it was nae hersell.

Said one of the Southron foragers,
"See ye yon lusty dame?
I wou'd nae gie muckle to thee, neebor,
To bring her back agen."

Then all the Southrons follow'd him,
And sure they were but four;
But he has drawn his trusty brand,
And slew them pair by pair.

He threw the pitchers frae his hands,
  And to the hills fled he,
Until he cam to a fair may,
  Was washin' on yon lea.

"What news, what news, ye weel far'd may?
  What news hae ye to gie?"
"Ill news, ill news," the fair may said,
  "Ill news I hae to thee.

"There is fyften English sogers
  Into that thatched inn,
Seeking Sir William Wallace;
  I fear that he is slain."

"Have ye any money in your pocket?
  Pray lend it unto me,
And when I come this way again,
  Repaid ye weel shall be."

She['s] put her hand in her pocket,
  And taen out shillings three;
He turn'd him right and round about,
  And thank'd the weel far'd may.

He had not gone a long rig length,
  A rig length and a span,
Until he met a bold beggar,
  As sturdy as cou'd gang.

"What news, what news, ye bold beggar?
  What news hae ye to gie?"
"O heavy news," the beggar said,
  "I hae to tell to thee.

"There is fyften English sogers,
  I heard them in yon inn,
Vowing to kill him Wallace;
  I fear the chief is slain."

"Will ye change apparell wi' me, auld man?
  Change your apparell for mine?
And when I come this way again,
  Ye'll be my ain poor man."

When he got on the beggar's coat,
  The pike staff in his hand,
He's dane him down to yon tavern,
  Where they were drinking wine.

"What news, what news, ye staff beggar?
  What news hae ye to gie?"
"I hae nae news, I heard nae news,
  As few I'll hae frae thee."

"I think your coat is ragged, auld man,
  But wou'd you wages win,
And tell where William Wallace is,
  We'll lay gold in your hand."

"Tell down, tell down your good red gold,
Upon the table head,
And ye sall William Wallace see,
Wi' the down-come of Robin Hood."

They had nae tauld the money down,
And laid it on his knee,
When candles, lamps, and candlesticks,
He on the floor gar'd flee.

And he has drawn his trusty brand,
And slew them one by one,
Then sat down at the table head,
And callèd for some wine.

The goodwife she ran but, ran but,
The goodman he ran ben,
The verra bairns about the fire
Were a' like to gang brain.

"Now if there be a Scotsman here,
He'll come and drink wi' me;
And if there be an English loun,
It is his time to flee."

The goodman was an Englishman,
And to the hills he ran,
The goodwife was a Scots woman,
And she came to his hand.

APPENDIX.

JOHNNY COCK. (See p. 11.)

FROM Fry's *Pieces of Ancient Poetry, from unpublished Manuscripts and scarce Books* (p. 51). Bristol, 1814.

"This ballad is taken from a modern quarto manuscript purchased at Glasgow of Messrs. Smith and Son in the year 1810, and containing several others, but written so corruptly as to be of little or no authority; appearing to be the text-book of some illiterate drummer, from its comprising the music of several regimental marches."

Fry did not observe that he was printing fragments of two different versions as one ballad. They are here separated.

I.

JOHNNY COCK, in a May morning,
  Sought water to wash his hands;
And he is awa to louse his dogs,
  That's tied wi iron bans,
That's tied wi iron bans.

His coat it is of the light Lincum green,
  And his breiks are of the same;

His shoes are of the American leather,
Silver buckles tying them.
Silver buckles, &c.

'He' hunted up, and so did 'he' down,
Till 'he' came to yon bush of scrogs,
And then to yon wan water,
Where he slept among his dogs.
* * * * *

Johnny Cock out-shot a' the foresters,
And out-shot a' the three;
Out shot a' the foresters,
Wounded Johnny aboun the bree.

" Woe be to you, foresters,
And an ill death may you die!
For there would not a wolf in a' the wood,
Have done the like to me.

" For ''twould ha' put its foot in the coll water,
And ha strinkled it on my bree;
And gin [it] that would not have done,
Would have gane and lett me be.

18–24. Finlay furnishes one beautiful stanza which belongs to this portion of the story, and, as that editor remarks, describes expressively the languor of approaching death.

There's no a bird in a' this foreste
Will do as meikle for me,
As dip its wing in the wan water
An straik it on my ee-bree.
Scottish Ballads, I. xxxi.

"I often took to my mother
The dandoo and the roe;
But now I'l take to my mother
Much sorrow and much woe.

"I often took to my mother
The dandoo and the hare;
But now I'l take to my mother
Much sorrow and much care."

II.

Fifteen foresters in the braid alow,
And they are wondrous fell;
To get a drop of Johnny's heart bluid,
They would sink a' their souls to hell.

Johnny Cock has gotten word of this,
And he is wondrous keen;
He['s] custan aff the red scarlet,
And on 'wi' the Linkum green.

And he is ridden oer muir and muss,
And over mountains high,
Till he came to yon wan water;
And there Johnny Cock did lie.

He's taen out a horn from his side,
And he blew both loud and shrill,
Till a' the fifteen foresters
Heard Johnny Cock blaw his horn.

They have sworn a bluidy oath,
  And they swore all in one,
That there was not a man among them a',
  Would blaw such a blast as yon.

And they have ridden oer muir and muss,
  And over mountains high,
Till they came to yon wan water,
  Where Johnny Cock did lie.

They have shotten little Johnny Cock,
  A little above the ee;
  *   *   *   *   *
  For doing the like to me.

" There's not a wolf in a' the wood
  Woud 'ha' done the like to me:
' She'd ha' dipped her foot in coll water,
  And strinkled above my ee,
And if I would have waked for that,
  ' She'd ha' gane and let me be.

" But fingers five, come here, [come here,]
  And faint heart fail me nought!
And silver strings, value me sma' things,
  Till I get all this vengeance rowght!"

He ha[s] shot a' the fifteen foresters,
  Left never a one but one;
And he broke the ribs a that anes side,
  And let him take tiding home.

29. word.   36. faint hearted.

They have ridden oer muir and muss,
And over mountains high,
Till they met wi 'an' old palmer,
Was walking along the way.

" What news, what news, old palmer,
What news have you to me ?"
" Yonder is one of the proudest wed sons
That ever my eyes did see.

* * * * *

" * * a bird in a' the wood
Could sing as I could say ;
It would go in to my mothers bower,
And bid her kiss me, and take me away."

THE LIFE AND DEATH OF SIR HUGH OF THE GRIME. (See p. 51.)

From Durfey's *Pills to purge Melancholy*, vi. 289.

THE same is printed in Ritson's *Ancient Songs* (ed. 1790), p. 192, from a collation of two black-letter copies, one in the collection of the Duke of Roxburgh, and " another in the hands of John Baynes, Esq." Several stanzas are corrupted, and the names are greatly disfigured. Ritson mentions in a note a somewhat different ballad on the same subject, beginning:—

" Good Lord John is a hunting gone."

53. bows.

As it befel upon one time,
About mid-summer of the year,
Every man was taxt of his crime,
For stealing the good Lord Bishop's mare.

The good Lord Screw sadled a horse,
And rid after the same serime;
Before he did get over the moss,
There was he aware of Sir Hugh of the Grime.

" Turn, O turn, thou false traytor,
Turn, and yield thyself unto me:
Thou hast stol'n the Lord Bishop's mare,
And now thinkest away to flee."

"No, soft, Lord Screw, that may not be;
Here is a broad sword by my side,
And if that thou canst conquer me,
The victory will soon be try'd."

" I ne'er was afraid of a traytor bold,
Altho' thy name be Hugh in the Grime;
I'll make thee repent thy speeches foul,
If day and life but give me time."

" Then do thy worst, good Lord Screw,
And deal your blows as fast as you can;
It will be try'd between me and you
Which of us two shall be the best man."

Thus as they dealt their blows so free,
And both so bloody at that time,
Over the moss ten yeomen they see,
Come for to take Sir Hugh in the Grime.

Sir Hugh set his back again[st] a tree,
And then the men compast him round;
His mickle sword from his hand did flee,
And then they brought Sir Hugh to the ground.

Sir Hugh of the Grime now taken is
And brought back to Garland town;
Then cry'd the good wives all in Garland town,
"Sir Hugh in the Grime, thou'st ne'er gang down."

The good Lord Bishop is come to town,
And on the bench is set so high;
And every man was tax'd to his crime,
At length he called Sir Hugh in the Grime.

"Here am I, thou false Bishop,
Thy humours all to fulfil;
I do not think my fact so great
But thou mayst put [it] into thy own will."

The quest of jury-men was call'd,
The best that was in Garland town;
Eleven of them spoke all in a breast,
"Sir Hugh in the Grime, thou'st ne'er gang down."

Then other questry-men was call'd,
The best that was in Rumary;
Twelve of them spoke all in a breast,
"Sir Hugh in the Grime, thou'st now guilty."

Then came down my good Lord Boles,
Falling down upon his knee;
"Five hundred pieces of gold will I give,
To grant Sir Hugh in the Grime to me."

"Peace, peace, my good Lord Boles,
And of your speeches set them by;
If there be eleven Grimes all of a name,
Then by my own honour they all should dye."

Then came down my good Lady Ward,
Falling low upon her knee;
"Five hundred measures of gold I'll give,
To grant Sir Hugh of the Grime to me."

"Peace, peace, my good Lady Ward,
None of your proffers shall him buy;
For if there be twelve Grimes all of a name,
By my own honour [they] all should dye."

Sir Hugh of the Grime's condemn'd to dye,
And of his friends he had no lack;
Fourteen foot he leapt in his ward,
His hands bound fast upon his back.

Then he look'd over his left shoulder,
To see whom he could see or 'spye;
Then was he aware of his father dear,
Came tearing his hair most pitifully.

"Peace, peace, my father dear,
And of your speeches set them by;
Tho' they have bereav'd me of my life,
They cannot bereave me of heaven so high."

He look'd over his right shoulder,
To see whom he could see or 'spye;
There was he aware of his mother dear,
Came tearing her hair most pitifully.

"Pray have me remember'd to Peggy my wife,
  As she and I walk'd over the moor,
She was the cause of the loss of my life,
  And with the old bishop she play'd the whore.

"Here, Johnny Armstrong, take thou my sword,
  That is made of the metal so fine,
And when thou com'st to the Border side,
  Remember the death of Sir Hugh of the Grime."

[JOHNIE ARMSTRANG, OR,] A NORTHERN BALLET.

From *Wit Restor'd*, p. 132.

THERE dwelt a man in faire Westmerland,
  Jonne Armestrong men did him call,
He had nither lands nor rents coming in,
  Yet he kept eight score men in his hall.

He had horse and harness for them all,
  Goodly steeds were all milke white,
O the golden bands an about their necks,
  And their weapons they were all alike.

Newes then was brought unto the king,
  That there was sicke a won as hee,
That lived lyke a bold out-law,
  And robbed all the north country.

11. syke.

The king he writt an a letter then
  A letter which was large and long,
He signed it with his owne hand,
  And he promised to doe him no wrong.

When this letter came Jonne untill,
  His heart it was as blythe as birds on the tree;
"Never was I sent for before any king,
  My father, my grandfather, nor none but mee.

"And if wee goe the king before,
  I would we went most orderly;
Every man of you shall have his scarlet cloak,
  Laced with silver laces three.

"Every won of you shall have his velvett coat,
  Laced with sillver lace so white;
O the golden bands an about your necks,
  Black hatts, white feathers, all alyke."

By the morrow morninge at ten of the clock,
  Towards Edenburough gon was hee,
And with him all his eight score men,
  Good lord, it was a goodly sight for to see!

When Jonne came befower the king,
  He fell downe on his knee;
"O pardon my soveraine leige," he said,
  "O pardon my eight score men and mee!"

"Thou shalt have no pardon, thou traytor strong,
  For thy eight score men nor thee;
For to-morrow morning by ten of the clock,
  Both thou and them shall hang on the gallow tree."

But Jonne looked over his left shoulder,
  Good Lord, what a grevious look looked hee!
Saying, "Asking grace of a graceles face—
  Why there is none for you nor me."

But Jonne had a bright sword by his side,
  And it was made of the mettle so free,
That had not the king stept his foot aside,
  He had smitten his head from his fair boddé.

Saying, " Fight on, my merry men all,
  And see that none of you be taine;
For rather then men shall say we were hanged,
  Let them report how we were slaine."

Then, God wott, faire Eddenburrough rose,
  And so besett poore Jonne[a] rounde,
That fowerscore and tenn of Jonnes best men,
  Lay gasping all upon the ground.

Then like a mad man Jonne laide about,
  And like a mad man then fought hee,
Untill a falce Scot came Jonne behinde,
  And runn him through the faire boddee.

Saying, " Fight on, my merry men all,
  And see that none of you be taine;
For I will stand by and bleed but a while,
  And then will I come and fight againe."

Newes then was brought to young Jonne Armestrong,
  As he stood by his nurses knee,
Who vowed if er'e he lived for to be a man,
  O th' the treacherous Scots reveng'd hee'd be.

LOUDOUN CASTLE. (See p. 149.)

FROM *The Ballads and Songs of Ayrshire*, First Series, p. 74, where it is taken from a *Statistical Account of the Parish of Loudoun.* The writer of the *Statistical Account* states that the old castle of Loudoun is supposed to have been destroyed by fire about 350 years ago. "The current tradition," he adds, "ascribes that event to the Clan Kennedy, and the remains of an old tower at Auchruglen, on the Galston side of the valley, is still pointed out as having been their residence."

IT fell about the Martinmas time,
  When the wind blew snell and cauld,
That Adam o' Gordon said to his men,
  "When will we get a hold?

"See [ye] not where yonder fair castle
  Stands on yon lily lee?
The laird and I hae a deadly feud,
  The lady fain would I see."

As she was up on the househead,
  Behold, on looking down,
She saw Adam o' Gordon and his men,
  Coming riding to the town.

The dinner was not well set down,
  Nor the grace was scarcely said,
Till Adam o' Gordon and his men
  About the walls were laid.

" It's fause now fa' thee, Jock my man ,
  Thou might a let me be ;
Yon man has lifted the pavement stone,
  An' let in the loun to me."

" Seven years I served thee, fair ladie,
  You gave me meat and fee ;
But now I am Adam o' Gordon's man,
  An' maun either do it or die."

" Come down, come down, my Lady Loudoun,
  Come thou down unto me ;
I'll wrap thee on a feather bed,
  Thy warrand I shall be."

" I'll no come down, I'll no come down,
  For neither laird nor loun,
Nor yet for any bloody butcher
  That lives in Altringham town.

" I would give the black," she says,
  " And so would I the brown,
If that Thomas, my only son,
  Could charge to me a gun."

Out then spake the Lady Margaret,
  As she stood on the stair,—
The fire was at her goud garters,
  The lowe was at her hair.

" I would give the black," she says,
  " And so would I the brown,

26. down thou.

For a drink of yon water,
  That rins by Galston Town."

Out then spake fair Anne,
  She was baith jimp and sma',
" O row me in a pair o' sheets,
  And tow me down the wa'."

" O hold thy tongue, thou fair Anne,
  And let thy talkin' be,
For thou must stay in this fair castle,
  And bear thy death with me."

" O mother," spoke the Lord Thomas,
  As he sat on the nurse's knee,
" O mother, give up this fair castle,
  Or the reek will worrie me."

" I would rather be burnt to ashes sma',
  And be cast on yon sea foam,
Before I'd give up this fair castle,
  And my lord so far from home.

" My good lord has an army strong,
  He's now gone o'er the sea;
He bade me keep this gay castle,
  As long as it would keep me.

" I've four-and-twenty brave milk kye
  Gangs on yon lily lee,
I'd give them a' for a blast of wind,
  To blaw the reek from me."

O pitie on yon fair castle,
  That's built with stone and lime,
But far mair pitie on Lady Loudoun,
  And all her children nine.

ROB ROY. (See p. 203.)

From *Select Scottish Songs, Ancient and Modern*, by Robert Burns, edited by Cromek, ii. 199.

ROB ROY from the Highlands cam,
  Unto the Lawlan' border,
To steal awa a gay ladie
  To haud his house in order.
He cam owre the lock o' Lynn,
  Twenty men his arms did carry;
Himsel gaed in, an' fand her out,
  Protesting he would marry.

"O will ye gae wi' me," he says,
  "Or will ye be my honey?
Or will ye be my wedded wife?
  For I love you best of any."
"I winna gae wi' you," she says,
  "Nor will I be your honey,
Nor will I be your wedded wife;
  You love me for my money."
* * * * *

But he set her on a coal-black steed,
  Himsel lap on behind her,

An' he's awa to the Highland hills,
  Whare her frien's they canna find her.
* * * * *

"Rob Roy was my father ca'd,
  Macgregor was his name, ladie;
He led a band o' heroes bauld,
  An' I am here the same, ladie.
Be content, be content,
  Be content to stay, ladie,
For thou art my wedded wife
  Until thy dying day, ladie.

"He was a hedge unto his frien's,
  A heckle to his foes, ladie,
Every one that durst him wrang,
  He took him by the nose, ladie.
I'm as bold, I'm as bold,
  I'm as bold, an more, ladie;
He that daurs dispute my word,
  Shall feel my guid claymore, ladie."

II.

From Maidment's *North Countrie Garland*, p. 44.

Rob Roy from the Highlands cam,
  Unto our Scottish border,
And he has stow'n a lady fair,
  To haud his house in order.

And when he cam, he surrounded the house,
  Twenty men their arms did carry,

And he has stow'n this lady fair,
  On purpose her to marry.

And when he cam, he surrounded the house;
  No tidings there cam before him,
Or else the lady would have been gone,
  For still she did abhor him.

Wi' murnfu' cries, and wat'ry eyes,
  Fast hauding by her mother,
Wi' murnfu' cries, and wat'ry eyes,
  They are parted frae each other.

Nae time he gied her to be dress'd,
  As ladies do when they're bride O,
But he hastened and hurried her awa',
  And he row'd her in his plaid O.

They rade till they cam to Ballyshine,
  At Ballyshine they tarried;
He bought to her a cotton gown,
  Yet ne'er would she be married.

Three held her up before the priest,
  Four carried her to bed O,
Wi' wat'ry eyes, and murnfu' sighs,
  When she behind was laid O.

* * * * *

" O be content, be content,
  Be content to stay, lady,
For ye are my wedded wife
  Unto my dying day, lady.

CHORUS.

Re content, be content,
Be content to stay, lady,
For ye are my wedded wife
Unto my dying day, lady.

"My father is Rob Roy called,
M'Gregor is his name, lady,
In all the country where he dwells,
He does succeed the fame, lady.

"My father he has cows and ewes,
And goats he has eneuch, lady,
And you, and twenty thousand merks,
Will make me a man complete, lady."

EPPIE MORRIE.

From Maidment's *North Countrie Garland*, p. 40.

"THIS ballad is probably much more than a century old, though the circumstances which have given rise to it were fortunately too common to preclude the possibility of its being of a later date. Although evidently founded on fact, the editor has not hitherto discovered the particular circumstances out of which it has originated."

FOUR and twenty Highland men
Came a' from Carrie side,
To steal awa' Eppie Morrie,
'Cause she would not be a bride.

Out it's cam her mother,
It was a moonlight night,
She could not see her daughter.
The sands they shin'd so bright.

"Haud far awa' frae me, mother,
Haud far awa' frae me;
There's not a man in a' Strathdon
Shall wedded be with me."

They have taken Eppie Morrie,
And horseback bound her on,
And then awa' to the minister,
As fast as horse could gang.

He's taken out a pistol,
And set it to the minister's breast;
"Marry me, marry me, minister,
Or else I'll be your priest."

"Haud far awa' frae me, good sir,
Haud far awa' frae me;
For there's not a man in a' Strathdon
That shall married be with me."

"Haud far awa' frae me, Willie,
Haud far awa' frae me;
For I darna avow to marry you,
Except she's as willing as ye."

They have taken Eppie Morrie,
Since better could nae be,
And they're awa' to Carrie side,
As fast as horse could flee.

Then mass was sung, and bells were rung,
And all were bound for bed,
Then Willie an' Eppie Morrie
In one bed they were laid.

"Haud far awa' frae me, Willie,
Haud far awa' frae me;
Before I'll lose my maidenhead,
I'll try my strength with thee."

She took the cap from off her head,
And threw it to the way;
Said, "Ere I lose my maidenhead,
I'll fight with you till day."

Then early in the morning,
Before her clothes were on,
In came the maiden of Scalletter,
Gown and shirt alone.

"Get up, get up, young woman,
And drink the wine wi' me;"
"You might have called me maiden,
I'm sure as leal as thee."

"Wally fa' you, Willie,
That ye could nae prove a man,
And taen the lassie's maidenhead;
She would have hired your han'."

"Haud far awa' frae me, lady,
Haud far awa' frae me;
There's not a man in a' Strathdon,
The day shall wed wi' me."

Soon in there came Belbordlane,
  With a pistol on every side;
"Come awa' hame, Eppie Morrie,
  And there you'll be my bride."

"Go get to me a horse, Willie,
  And get it like a man,
And send me back to my mother,
  A maiden as I cam.

"The sun shines o'er the westlin hills,
  By the light lamp of the moon,
Just saddle your horse, young John Forsyth,
  And whistle, and I'll come soon."

MACPHERSON'S RANT.

This ballad, worthy of a hangman's pen, was first printed in Herd's *Scottish Songs*, i. 161. It is found, mutilated and altered, with the title of *Macpherson's Lament*, in the *Thistle of Scotland*, p. 52.

The story of Macpherson is given as follows by a writer in the *New Monthly Magazine*, vol. i. p. 142, cited by Chambers, *Scottish Songs*, i. 84.

"James Macpherson was born of a beautiful gipsy, who, at a great wedding, attracted the notice of a half-intoxicated Highland gentleman. He acknowledged the child, and had him reared in his house, until he lost his life in bravely pursuing a hostile clan, to recover a spreach of cattle taken from Badenoch.

The gipsy woman, hearing of this disaster, in her rambles the following summer, came and took away her boy; but she often returned with him, to wait upon his relations and clansmen, who never failed to clothe him well, besides giving money to his mother. He grew up to beauty, strength, and stature, rarely equalled. His sword is still preserved at Duff House, a residence of the Earl of Fife, and few men of our day could carry, far less wield it, as a weapon of war; and if it must be owned that his prowess was debased by the exploits of a free-booter, it is certain, no act of cruelty, no robbery of the widow, the fatherless, or distressed, and no murder, were ever perpetrated under his command. He often gave the spoils of the rich to relieve the poor; and all his tribe were restrained from many atrocities of rapine by the awe of his mighty arm. Indeed, it is said that a dispute with an aspiring and savage man of his tribe, who wished to rob a gentleman's house while his wife and two children lay on the bier for interment, was the cause of his being betrayed to the vengeance of the law. The magistrates of Aberdeen were exasperated at Macpherson's escape, and bribed a girl in that city to allure and deliver him into their hands. There is a platform before the jail, at the top of a stair, and a door below. When Macpherson's capture was made known to his comrades by the frantic girl, who had been so credulous as to believe the magistrates only wanted to hear the wonderful performer on the violin, his cousin, Donald Macpherson, a gentleman of Herculean powers, did not disdain to come from Badenoch, and to join a gipsy, Peter Brown, in liberating the prisoner. On a market-day they brought several assistants; and swift horses were stationed at a convenient distance. Donald Macpherson and Peter Brown forced the jail; and while Peter Brown went to help the heavily-fettered James Macpherson in moving away, Donald Macpherson guarded the jail-door with a drawn sword. Many persons assembled at the market had experienced James Macpherson's humanity, or had shared his bounty; and they crowded round the jail as in mere curiosity, but, in fact, to obstruct the civil authorities in their attempts to prevent a rescue. A butcher, however, was resolved to detain Macpherson, expecting a large recompense from the magistrates; he sprung up the stairs, and leaped from the platform upon Donald Macpherson, whom he dashed to the ground by the force and weight of his body. Donald Macpherson soon recovered, to make a desperate resistance; and the combatants tore off each other's clothes. The butcher got a glimpse of his dog upon the platform, and called him to his aid; but Macpherson, with admirable presence of mind, snatched up his own plaid, which lay near, and threw it over the butcher, thus misleading the instinct of his canine adversary. The dog darted with fury upon the plaid, and terribly lacerated his master's thigh. In the mean time, James Macpherson had been carried out by Peter Brown, and was soon joined by Donald Macpherson, who was quickly covered by some friendly spectator with a hat and great coat. The magistrates ordered webs from the shops to be drawn across the Gallowgate; but Donald Macpherson cut them asunder with his sword, and James, the late prisoner, got off on horseback. He was, some time after, betrayed by a man of his own tribe;

and was the last person executed at Banff, previous to the abolition of hereditable jurisdiction. He was an admirable performer on the violin; and his talent for composition is still evidenced by Macpherson's Rant, and Macpherson's Pibroch. He performed these tunes at the foot of the fatal tree; and then asked if he had any friend in the crowd to whom a last gift of his instrument would be acceptable. No man had hardihood to claim friendship with a delinquent, in whose crimes the acknowledgment might implicate an avowed acquaintance. As no friend came forward, Macpherson said, the companion of so many gloomy hours should perish with him; and, breaking the violin over his knees, he threw away the fragments. Donald Macpherson picked up the neck of the violin, which to this day is preserved, as a valuable memento, by the family of Cluny, chieftain of the Macphersons."

Burns's magnificent death-song, *McPherson's Farewell*, is too well known to require more than an allusion.

I'VE spent my time in rioting,
Debauch'd my health and strength;
I've pillag'd, plunder'd, murdered,
But now, alas! at length,
I'm brought to punishment direct,
Pale death draws near to me;
This end I never did project,
To hang upon a tree.

To hang upon a tree! a tree!
That curs'd unhappy death!

Like to a wolf to worried be,
And choaked in the breath.
My very heart would surely break,
When this I think upon,
Did not my courage singular
Bid pensive thoughts begone.

No man on earth that draweth breath,
More courage had than I;
I dar'd my foes unto their face,
And would not from them fly.
This grandeur stout, I did keep out,
Like Hector, manfullie:
Then wonder one like me, so stout,
Should hang upon a tree!

Th' Egyptian band I did command,
With courage more by far,
Than ever did a general
His soldiers in the war.
Being fear'd by all, both great and small,
I liv'd most joyfullie:
O! curse upon this fate of mine,
To hang upon a tree!

As for my life, I do not care,
If justice would take place,
And bring my fellow plunderers
Unto this same disgrace.
For Peter Brown, that notour loon,
Escap'd and was made free;
O! curse upon this fate of mine,
To hang upon a tree!

Both law and justice buried are,
  And fraud and guile succeed;
The guilty pass unpunished,
  If money intercede.
The Laird of Grant, that Highland saint,
  His mighty majestie,
He pleads the cause of Peter Brown,
  And lets Macpherson die.

The destiny of my life, contriv'd
  By those whom I oblig'd,
Rewarded me much ill for good,
  And left me no refuge.
For Braco Duff, in rage enough,
  He first laid hands on me;
And if that death would not prevent,
  Avenged would I be.

As for my life, it is but short,
  When I shall be no more;
To part with life I am content,
  As any heretofore.
Therefore, good people all, take heed,
  This warning take by me,
According to the lives you lead,
  Rewarded you shall be

BOOK VIII.

THE FLEMISH INSURRECTION.

THE Flemings, having abandoned their legitimate sovereign and attached themselves to Philip the Fair, found at last cause to repent. In 1301, two citizens of Bruges, Peter de Koning, a draper, and John Breydel, a butcher, stirred up their townsmen to revolt, and drove out the French garrison. The next year, the Count d'Artois, with a superb army, was defeated by the insurgents at the battle of Courtrai.

This ballad is found in MS. Harl. No. 2253, "of the reign of Edw. II." and has been printed in Ritson's *Ancient Songs* (i. 51), and in Wright's *Political Songs*, p. 187. We have adopted the text of the latter.

LUSTNETH, lordinges, bothe yonge ant olde,
Of the Freynsshe men that were so proude ant bolde,
Hou the Flemmysshe men bohten hem ant solde,
Upon a Wednesday.
Betere hem were at home in huere londe,
Then for te seche Flemmysshe by the see stronde,
Whare thourh moni Frenshe wyf wryngeth hire honde,
Ant singeth weylaway.

The Kyng of Fraunce made statuz newe,
In the lond of Flaundres among false ant trewe,
That the commun of Bruges ful sore con arewe,
Ant seiden amonges hem,

"Gedere we us togedere hardilyche at ene,
Take we the bailifs bi tuenty ant by tene,
Clappe we of the hevedes anonen o the grene,
Ant caste we y the fen."

The webbes ant the fullaris assembleden hem alle,
Ant makeden huere consail in huere commune halle;
Token Peter Conyng huere kyng to calle,
Ant beo huere cheventeyn.
Hue nomen huere rouncyns out of the stalle,
Ant closeden the toun withinne the walle;
Sixti baylies ant ten hue maden adoun falle,
Ant moni an other sweyn.

Tho wolde the baylies that were come from Fraunce,
Dryve the Flemisshe that made the destaunce;
Hue turnden hem ayeynes with suerd ant with launce,
Stronge men ant lyht.
Y telle ou for sothe, for al huere bobaunce,
Ne for the avowerie of the Kyng of Fraunce,
Tuenti score ant fyve haden ther meschaunce,
By day ant eke by nyht.

Sire Jakes de Seint Poul, yherde hou hit was;
Sixtene hundred of horsemen asemblede o the gras;
He wende toward Bruges *pas pur pas*,
With swithe gret mounde
The Flemmysshe yherden telle the cas,
Agynneth to clynken huere basyns of bras,
Ant al hem to-dryven ase ston doth the glas,
Ant fellen hem to grounde.

15. anonen. R. an oven. W.

Sixtene hundred of horsmen hede ther herc fyn;
Hue leyyen y the stretes ystyked ase swyn,
Ther hue loren huere stedes ant mony rouncyn,
Thourh huere oune prude.
Sire Jakes ascapede, by a coynte gyn,
Out at one posterne ther me solde wyn,
Out of the fyhte hom to ys yn,
In wel muchele drede.

Tho the Kyng of Fraunce yherde this, anon,
Assemblede he is doussé-pers everuchon,
The proude eorl of Artoys ant other mony on,
To come to Paris.
The barouns of Fraunce thider conne gon,
Into the paleis that paved is with ston,
To jugge the Flemmisshe to bernen ant to slon,
Thourh the flour de lis.

Thenne seide the Kyng Philip, "Lustneth nou to me;
Myn eorles ant my barouns, gentil ant fre:
Goth, faccheth me the traytours ybounde to my kne;
Hastifliche ant blyve."
Tho suor the Eorl of Seint Poul, "*Par la goule dé*,
We shule facche the rybaus wher thi wille be,
Ant drawen hem [with] wilde hors out of the countrè,
By thousendes fyve."

"Sire Rauf Devel," sayth the Eorl of Boloyne,
"*Nus ne lerrum en vie chanoun ne moyne;*
Wende we forth anon ritht withoute eny assoygne,
Ne no lyves man.
We shule flo the Conyng, ant make roste is loyne;
The word shal springen of him into Coloyne,

So hit shal to Acres ant into Sesoyne,
Ant maken him ful wan."

Sevene eorls ant fourti barouns y-tolde,
Fiftene hundred knyhtes, proude ant swythe bolde,
Sixti thousent swyers amonge yunge ant olde,
Flemmisshe to take.
The Flemmisshe hardeliche hem come to-yeynes;
This proude Freinsshe eorles, huere knyhtes ant huere sweynes,
Aquelleden ant slowen, by hulles ant by pleynes,
Al for huere kynges sake.

This Frenshe come to Flaundres so liht so the hare;
Er hit were mydnyht hit fel hem to care;
Hue were laht by the net so bryd is in snare,
With rouncin ant with stede.
The Flemmisshe hem dabbeth o the het bare;
Hue nolden take for huem raunsoun ne ware;
Hue doddeth of huere hevedes, fare so hit fare,
Ant thareto haveth hue nede.

Thenne seyth the Eorl of Artois, "Y yelde me to the,
Peter Conyng, by thi nome, yef thou art hende ant fre,
That y ne have no shame ne no vylté,
That y ne be noud ded."
Thenne swor a bocher, "By my leauté,
Shalt thou ner more the kyng of Fraunce se,
Ne in the toun of Bruges in prisone be;
Thou woldest spene bred."

Ther hy were knulled y the putfalle,
This eorles ant barouns ant huere knyhtes alle;

Huere ledies huem mowe abide in boure ant in halle
Wel longe.
For hem mot huere kyng other knyhtes calle,
Other stedes taken out of huere stalle:
Ther hi habbeth dronke bittrere then the galle,
Upon the drue londe.

When the Kyng of Fraunce yherde this tydynge,
He smot doun is heved, is honden gon he wrynge:
Thourhout al Fraunce the word bygon to sprynge,
Wo wes huem tho!
Muche wes the sorewe ant the wepinge
That wes in al Fraunce among olde ant yynge;
The mest part of the lond bygon for te synge
"Alas ant weylawo!"

Awey, thou yunge pope! whet shal the to rede?
Thou hast lore thin cardinals at thi meste nede;
Ne keverest thou hem nevere for nones kunnes mede,
For sothe y the telle.
Do the forth to Rome, to amende thi misdede;
Bide gode halewen, hue lete the betere spede;
Bote thou worche wysloker, thou losest lont ant lede,
The coroune wel the felle.

Alas, thou seli Fraunce! for the may thunche shome,
That ane fewe fullaris maketh ou so tome;
Sixti thousent on a day hue maden fot-lome,
With eorl ant knyht.
Herof habbeth the Flemysshe suithe god game,
Ant suereth by Seint Omer ant eke bi Seint Jame,
Yef hy ther more cometh, hit falleth huem to shame,
With huem for te fyht.

I telle ou for sothe, the bataille thus bigon
Bituene Fraunce ant Flaundres, hou hue weren fon;
Vor Vrenshe the Eorl of Flaundres in prison heden ydon,
With tresoun untrewe.
Ye[f] the Prince of Walis his lyf habbé mote,
Hit falleth the Kyng of Fraunce bittrore then the sote;
Bote he the rathere therof welle do bote,
Wel sore hit shal hym rewe.

THE EXECUTION OF SIR SIMON FRASER.

On the 27th of March, 1306, Robert Bruce was crowned king at Scone. Immediately thereupon, King Edward the First sent the Earl of Pembroke, Aymer de Valence, to Scotland, to suppress what he called the rebellion in that kingdom. Pembroke attacked Bruce in his cantonments at Methven (or Kirkenclif) near Perth, and dispersed his small army, taking several prisoners of great consequence. Among them was Sir Simon Fraser, or Frisel, whose cruel fate is narrated in the following ballad.

This piece has been printed in Ritson's *Ancient Songs* (i. 28), and in Wright's *Political Songs*, p. 212, and is extracted from the same MS. as the preceding ballad.

Lystneth, lordynges, a newe song ichulle bigynne,
Of the traytours of Scotlond, that take beth wyth gynne;

Mon that loveth falsnesse, and nule never blynne,
Sore may him drede the lyf that he is ynne,
Ich understonde:
Selde wes he glad
That never nes a-sad
Of nythe ant of onde.

That y sugge by this Scottes that bueth nou to-drawe,
The hevedes o Londone-brugge, whosé con y-knawe;
He wenden han buen kynges, ant seiden so in sawe;
Betere hem were han y-be barouns, ant libbe in Godes lawe
Wyth love.
Whosé hateth soth ant ryht,
Lutel he douteth Godes myht,
The heye kyng above.

To warny alle the gentilmen that bueth in Scotlonde,
The Waleis wes to-drawe, seththe he wes an-honge,
Al quic biheveded, ys bowels ybrend,
The heved to Londone-brugge wes send,
To abyde.
After Simond Frysel,
That wes traytour ant fykell,
Ant y-cud ful wyde.

Sire Edward oure kyng, that ful ys of pieté,
The Waleis quarters sende to is oune contré,
On four-half to honge, huere myrour to be,
Theropon to thenche, that monie myhten se,
Ant drede.
Why nolden he be war
Of the bataile of Donbar,
Hou evele hem con spede ?

Bysshopes ant barouns come to the kynges pes,
Ase men that weren fals, fykel, ant les,
Othes hue him sworen in stude ther he wes,
To buen him hold ant trewe for alles cunnes res,
Thrye,
That hue ne shulden ayeyn him go,
So hue were temed tho;
Weht halt hit to lye?

To the kyng Edward hii fasten huere fay;
Fals wes here foreward so forst is in May,
That sonne from the southward wypeth away;
Moni proud Scot therof mene may
To yere.
Nes never Scotlond
With dunt of monnes hond
Allinge aboht so duere.

The bisshop of Glascou y chot he wes ylaht,
The bisshop of Seint-Andrè, bothe he beth ycaht,
The abbot of Scon with the kyng nis nout saht,
Al here purpos ycome hit ys to naht,
Thurh ryhte:
Hii were unwis
When hii thohte pris
Ayeyn huere kyng to fyhte.

Thourh consail of thes bisshopes ynemned byfore,
Sire Robert the Bruytz furst kyng wes ycore;
He mai everuche day ys fon him se byfore,
Yef hee mowen him hente, i chot he bith forlore,
Sauntz fayle.
Soht for te sugge,

Duere he shal abugge
That he bigon batayle.

Hii that him crounede proude were ant bolde,
Hii maden kyng of somer, so hii ner ne sholde,
Hii setten on ys heved a croune of rede golde,
Ant token him a kyneyerde, so me kyng sholde,
To deme.
Tho he wes set in see,
Lutel god couthe he
Kyneriche to yeme.

Nou kyng Hobbe in the mures yongeth,
For te come to toune nout him ne longeth;
The barouns of Engelond, myhte hue him grype,
He him wolde techen on Englysshe to pype,
Thourh streynthe:
Ne be he ner so stout,
Yet he bith ysoht out
O brede ant o leynthe.

Sire Edward of Carnarvan, (Jhesu him save ant see!)
Sire Emer de Valence, gentil knyht ant free,
Habbeth ysuore huere oht that, *par la grace dée*,
Hee wolleth ous delyvren of that false contree,
Yef hii conne.
Muche hath Scotlond forlore,
Whet alast, whet bifore,
Ant lutel pris wonne.

66. Bruce's wife, it is said, replied to her husband, when he was boasting of his royal rank, "You are indeed a summer king, but you will scarce be a winter one," alluding to the ephemeral sovereignty of the Lord of the May.

Nou i chulle fonge ther ich er let,
Ant tellen ou of Frisel, ase ich ou byhet.
In the batayle of Kyrkenclyf Frysel wes ytake;
Ys continaunce abatede eny bost to make
Biside Strivelyn;
Knyhtes ant sweynes,
Fremen ant theynes,
Monye with hym.

So hii weren byset on everuche halve,
Somme slaye were, ant sommè dreynte hemselve;
Sire Johan of Lyndeseye nolde nout abyde,
He wod into the water, his feren him bysyde,
To adrenche.
Whi nolden hii be war?
Ther nis non ayeyn star:—
Why nolden hy hem bythenche?

This wes byfore seint Bartholomeus masse,
That Frysel wes ytake, were hit more other lasse;
To sire Thomas of Multon, gentil baron ant fre,
Ant to sire Johan Jose, bytake tho wes he
To honde:
He wes yfetered weel,
Bothe with yrn ant wyth steel,
To bringen of Scotlonde.

Sone therafter the tydynge to the kyng com;
He him sende to Londone, with mony armed grom;
He com yn at Newegate, y telle yt ou aplyht,
A gerland of leves on ys hed ydyht,
Of grene;
For he shulde ben yknowe,

Bothe of heye ant of lowe,
For treytour, y wene.

Yfetered were ys legges under his horse wombe,
Bothe with yrn ant with stel mankled were ys honde,
A gerland of peruenke set on his heved;
Muche wes the poer that him wes byreved
In londe:
So god me amende,
Lutel he wende
So be broht in honde.

Sire Herbert of Norham, feyr knyht ant bold,
For the love of Frysel ys lyf wes ysold;
A wajour he made, so hit wes ytold,
Ys heved of to smhyte, yef me him brohte in hold,
Wat so bytyde:
Sory wes he thenne
Tho he myhte him kenne
Thourh the toun ryde.

Thenne seide ys scwyer a word anon ryht,
" Sire, we beth dede, ne helpeth hit no wyht,"
(Thomas de Boys the scwyer wes to nome,)
" Nou, y chot, our wajour turneth us to grome,

129. He was one of the Scottish prisoners in the Tower; and is said to have been so confident of the safety or success of Sir Simon Fraser, that he had offered to lay his own head on the block, if that warrior suffered himself to be taken; and (however involuntarily) it seems he kept his word. Vide M. West. 460.—Ritson. MS. Morham.

So ybate."
Y do ou to wyte,
Here heved wes of-smyte,
Byfore the Tour-gate.

This wes on oure Levedy even, for sothe ych understonde;
The justices seten for the knyhtes of Scotlonde,
Sire Thomas of Multone, an hendy knyht ant wys,
Ant sire Rauf of Sondwyche, that muchel is hold in prys,
Ant sire Johan Abel;
Mo y mihte telle by tale,
Bothe of grete ant of smale,
Ye knowen suythe wel.

Thenne saide the justice, that gentil is ant fre,
" Sire Simond Frysel, the kynges traytour hast thou be,
In water ant in londe, that monie myhten se.
What sayst thou thareto, hou wolt thou quite the?
Do say."
So foul he him wiste,
Nede waron truste
For to segge nay.

Ther he wes ydemed, so hit wes londes lawe;
For that he wes lordswyk, furst he wes to-drawe;
Upon a retheres hude forth he wes ytuht:
Sum while in ys time he wes a modi knyht,

145. 7th September.

147. Sir Thomas Multon was one of the justices of the King's Bench in 1289. Sir Ralph Sandwich was made Baron of the Exchequer in 1312.—Ritson. 148. MS. told.

In huerte.
Wickednesse ant sunne,
Hit is lutel wunne
That maketh the body smerte.

For al is grete poer, yet he wes ylaht;
Falsnesse ant swykedom, al hit geth to naht;
Tho he wes in Scotlond, lutel wes ys thoht
Of the harde jugement that him wes bysoht
In stounde.
He wes foursithe forswore
To the kyng ther bifore,
Ant that him brohte to grounde.

With feteres ant with gyves i chot he wes to-drowe,
From the Tour of Londone, that monie myhte knowe,
In a curtel of burel, a selkethe wyse,
Ant a gerland on ys heved of the newe guyse,
Thurh Cheepe;
Moni mon of Engelond
For to se Symond
Thideward con lepe.

Tho he com to galewes, furst he wes anhonge,
Al quic byheveded, thah him thohte longe;

175. Sir Simon was one of those whom King Edward brought out of Scotland in 1296, when that kingdom was first subdued. He remained a close prisoner about eight months, and was then freed, on entering into the usual engagement with the conqueror, to which, however, it is certain he did not think proper to adhere; esteeming it, perhaps, more sinful to keep such a forced obligation than to take it. Abercrombie, i. 552.—Ritson.

Seththe he wes y-opened, is boweles ybrend,
The heved to Londone-brugge wes send,
To shonde:
So ich ever mote the,
Sumwhile wende he
Ther lutel to stonde.

He rideth thourh the sité, as y telle may,
With gomen ant wyth solas, that wes here play;
To Londone-brugge hee nome the way,
Moni wes the wyves chil that theron laketh a day,
Ant seide, Alas,
That he wes ibore,
Ant so villiche forlore,
So feir mon ase he was!

Nou stont the heved above the tu-brugge,
Faste bi Waleis, soth for te sugge;
After socour of Scotlond longe he mowe prye,
Ant after help of Fraunce, (wet halt hit to lye?)
Ich wene.
Betere him were in Scotlond,
With is ax in ys hond,
To pleyen o the grene.

Ant the body hongeth at the galewes faste,
With yrnene claspes longe to laste;
For te wyte wel the body, ant Scottysh to garste,
Foure ant twenti ther beoth to sothe ate laste,
By nyhte:
Yef eny were so hardi
The body to remuy,
Al so to dyhte.

Were sire Robert the Bruytz ycome to this londe,
Ant the erl of Asseles, that harde is an honde,
Alle the other pouraille, forsothe ich understonde,
Mihten be ful blythe ant thonke godes sonde,
        Wyth ryhte;
    Thenne myhte uch mon
    Bothe riden ant gon
        In pes withoute vyhte.

The traytours of Scotland token hem to rede
The barouns of Engelond to brynge to dede:
Charles of Fraunce, so moni mon tolde,
With myht ant with streynthe hem helpe wolde,
        His thonkes.
    Tprot, Scot, for thi strif!
    Hang up thyn hachet ant thi knyf,
    Whil him lasteth the lyf
        With the longe shonkes.

218. The Earl of Athol, John de Strathbogie. Attempting to escape by sea, he was driven back by a storm, taken, and conveyed to London, where he was tried, condemned, and, with circumstances of great barbarity, put to death, 7th, &c. November, 1306. (M. West. 461.) Which proves the present ballad to have been composed between that time and the 7th of September preceding.—Ritson.

GLOSSARY.

☞ Figures placed after words denote the pages in which they occur.

---

ablins, *perhaps.*
aboon, abune, *above.*
abugge, *aby, pay for.*
adrenche, *drown.*
ae, *one;* first ae, *first.*
agynneth, *begin.*
ahint, *behind.*
airns, *irons.*
airt, *quarter of the compass, direction.*
alacing, *saying alas.*
alane, mine, *alone by myself.*
alast, *latterly.*
alles, *all.*
allinge, *altogether.*
alow, 245, *below.*
al so, *at once.*
amense, *amends.*
American leather, 244?
anew, *enough.*
an honde, 283, *in hand.*
anis, *once.*
aplyht, 273, a particle of confirmation, *indeed, on my word,* &c.
aquelleden, *killed.*
arewe, 269, *rue, feel aggrieved by.*
assoygne, 271, *delay*: (lines 66, 67, should probably be transposed.)
asteir, *astir, moved,* (his anger.)
avow, 261, *consent, undertake.*
avowerie, *protection, support.*
awin, *own.*
awsome, *frightful.*
ayeyn, *against:* 278, v. 103, a word seems to have dropped out. The sense is, *there is no resisting the stars.* Wright reads *stare.*
ayont, *beyond, on one side of.*

bangisters, *violent and lawless people, those that have the upper hand, victors.*
basnet, *helmet.*
batts, *beating.*
beet, 90, *help.*
ben, *in.*

bent, *coarse grass; open country*, covered with the same.
benty, *covered with the coarse grass called bent;* benty-line, 13?
beseen, weil, 132, *well appointed.*
bide, 273, *pray to.*
bigged, *built.*
biheveded, *beheaded.*
billie, *comrade.*
birk, *birch.*
birst, (*burst*) *fray.*
blan, *stopped.*
blink, 49, *glanced.*
blive, *quickly.*
bobaunce, *vanity, presumption.*
bode, *bid.*
borrow, *rescue.*
bot and, *and also.*
bote, 274, *amends;* bote, no, *not better off.*
boun, *ready, gone.*
brae, *hill-side.*
braid, 245, qy. corrupt?
brain, gang, *go mad.*
brank, 124, *prance, caper.*
branks, *a rude sort of bridle of rope and wood*, used by country people.
braw, bra', *brave, fine.*
brayd on, 32, *move on* (rapidly).
breast, 249, *voice.*
breasting, *springing forward.*
brecham, *collar of a working horse.*
brede, o, ant o leynthe, *in breadth and in length, far and wide.*
breek, *breeches;* 70, breek-thigh, *the side pocket of the breeches.*
brie, *brow.*
broked cow, *a cow that has black spots mixed with white in her face.*
broken men, *outlawed men.*
browhead, *forehead.*
brugge, *bridge.*
brusten, *burst.*
bryd, *bird.*
bryttled, *cut up.*
bueth, *be.*
bufft coat, *leather coat.*
bund, *bound.*
burel, *sackcloth.*
burn, *brook.*
busk, *make ready.*
buss, *bush.*
bussing, 137, *covering* (stolen from the packs).
but, *out;* 236, but the floor, *across the floor out of the room*, or *to the outer part of the house.*
by (sometimes) *besides.*
byhet, *promised.*
byres, byris, *barns, cowhouses.*
bysoht, *prepared for.*
bytake, *committed.*
bythenche, *bethink.*

ca' *call.*
ca', 90, *drive.*
carle, *churl, fellow.*
carpit, *talked, told stories.*
ca's, *calves.*
cauler, *cool.*

cess, *tax, black-mail.*
cheventeyn, *chieftain.*
chot, *wot, know.*
chulle, *shall.*
claes, *clothes.*
clanked, *gave a smart stroke.*
cleugh, *a rugged ascent.*
closs, 191, *area before the house, (close.)*
coll, *cool.*
coman, *command.*
con, 269, *began.*
conquess, *conquer.*
continaunce, *countenance.*
corbie, *crow.*
corn-caugers, *corn-carriers*, or *dealers.*
cost, 135, *loss, risk.*
could, 102, *began.*
coune, *began.*
courtrie, *band of courtiers.*
couthe, *knew.*
cowte, *colt.*
coynte, *quaint, cunning.*
crabit, *crabbed.*
cracking, *boasting.*
crooks, *the windings of a river, the space of ground closed in on one side by these windings.*
crouse, *brisk, bold.*
cumber, to red the, *quell the tumult.*
cunnes, *kinds.*
curch, *kerchief, coif.*
cure, 214, *care, pains.*
curtel, 281, *shirt, gown.*
custan, cast.
dae, *doe.*
dandoo, 245, apparently should be *dun doe.*
dane, *done, taken.*
dang, *beat.*
daw, *dawn.*
de, (Fr.) *God.*
dede, *dealt.*
dee, *die.*
deid, *death.*
deme, *adjudge.*
destaunce, *disturbance.*
ding down, *beat down.*
dints, *blows.*
doddeth, 272, *lop.*
dool, *grief.*
dought, *could, was able.*
dour, *hard.*
douse, *quiet, mild.*
doussé-pers, (Fr. douze pairs) *gallant knights.*
douteth, *feareth.*
dow, *can, are able;* downa, *cannot.*
down-come of Robin Hood, 242, *as quick as R. H. would knock one down?* or *pay down?*
dreigh, (*tedious, long*) *high.*
dreynte, drowned.
drie, *bear, endure.*
drifts, 100, *droves.*
drivand, *driving.*
drue, *dry.*
drunkily, *merrily.*
drury, *treasure.*
dub, *pool, pond.*
duere, *dear.*
dule, *sorrow.*

dunt, *dint*, *stroke*.
dyhte, 282, *dispose of*.

e'en, 93, *even, put in comparison*.
een, *eyes*.
elshin, *shoemaker's awl*.
ene, 270, *even*.
enew, *enough*.
er, *before*.
ettled, *designed*.
everuche, *every;* everuchon, *every one*.

falla, *fellow*.
fand, *found*.
fang, *catch*.
fankit, *entangled*, *obstructed;* here, *so fixed that it could not be drawn*.
fared, *went*.
fasten, 276, *plight*.
fay, *faith*.
fear't, *frightened*.
fecht, *fight*.
fee, *income*, *property*, *wages*.
feid, *feud*.
feir, 222, *sound*, *unhurt*.
feiries, *comrades*.
fell, *high pasture land*.
fend, *defence*.
feren, *comrades*.
ferly, *wonder*.
fet, *foot*.
fie, *predestined*.
fiend, 9, i. e. *the devil a thing*.
fit, *foot*.
flain, *arrows*.
flatlies, *flat*.
fley, *fright*.
flinders, *fragments*.
flo, *flay*.
fon, 274, *foes*.
fonge, *take up*.
forbode, over God's, (*on God's prohibition*), *God forbid*.
forehammer, *the large hammer which strikes before the small one*, *sledge-hammer*.
foreward, *covenant*.
forfaulted, *forfeited*.
forfend, *forbid*.
forfoughen (i. e. forfoughten) *tired out*.
forst, *frost*.
fot-lome, *foot-lame*.
fou, *full* (*of drink*).
four-half, on, *in quarters*.
foursithe, *four times*.
fow, 219, *full?*
frae hand, *forthwith*.
freits, *omens*.
frith, *wood*.
furs, *furrows*.
fyn, *end*.

gar, *make*, *let*.
garste, 282, (should probably be gast) *frighten away*.
gaun, *going*.
gavelocks, (*javelins*) *iron crows*.
gear, *goods*, *property;* 16, *spoil*.
ged, *went*.
geir, same as gear.
genzie, *engine of war*.
gifted, 31, *given away*.
gilt, *gold*.
gin, *if*.

gin, *trick.*
gleed, *red-hot coal, a glowing bar of iron.*
gloamin', *twilight.*
gomen, 282, *game, mockery.*
goud, *gold.*
goule, (Fr.) *throat.*
graith, *armor.*
graith, *make ready;* graithed, *armed.*
grat, *wept.*
green, *yearn, long.*
greeting, *weeping.*
gripet, *seized.*
grom, *groom, man.*
grome, 279, *sorrow.*
gryming, *sprinkling.*
guided, 172, *treated.*
gynne, *trap.*

had, haud, *hold.*
haif, *have.*
hail, 133, (*vigorous*, and so) *boisterous?*
halewen, *saints.*
halt, 276, 282, *profits?*
halve, *side.*
haly, *holy.*
happers, *hoppers.*
hardilyche, *boldly.*
harpit, *harped.*
harried, *plundered.*
hastifliche, *hastily.*
haud, *hold, keep.*
he, 282, *they.*
head, 117, *assemblage.*
heckle, *a hatchel, flax-comb.*
hem, *them.*
hende, hendy, *gentle.*
hente, *caught.*
herry, *harry, spoil.*
he's, *he shall.*
het, *head.*
het, *hot.*
heugh, *a ragged steep*, sometimes, *a glen with steep overhanging sides.*
heved, *head.*
hi, *they.*
hie, *high.*
hirst, *a barren hill.*
hold, 276, *faithful.*
hope, houp, *a sloping hollow between two hills.*
hostage house, 233, *inn.*
how, *pull.*
howm, *a plain on a river side.*
hue, *they;* huem, *them;* huere, *their.*
hulles, *hills.*

ibore, *born.*
ich, *I.*
ichulle, *I shall.*
ilka, *every.*
intill, *in.*
is, *his.*
I'se, *I will.*

jack, *a short coat plated with small pieces of iron.*
jeopardy, 223, *adventure.*
jimp, *slender.*
jugge, 271, *condemn.*

keekit, *peeped.*
kend, *known.*
kettrin, *cateran, thieving.*

keverest, 273, *recoverest.*
kilted, *tucked.*
kinnen, *rabbits.*
kirns, *churns.*
Kirsty, *Christy.*
knapscap, *head-piece.*
know, *knoll.*
knulled, 272, *pushed, beaten (with the knuckles).*
kunnes, *kinds.*
kyne-yerde, *king's wand* or *sceptre.*
kyneriche, *kingdom.*

laht, *caught.*
laigh, *low.*
langsome, *tedious.*
lap, *wrap up.*
lave, *rest.*
law, *low.*
lawing, *scot, reckoning.*
lay, *lea.*
layne, *conceal.*
leal, leel, *loyal, true, chaste.*
lear, *lore.*
leauté, *loyalty.*
lede, *people.*
lee, *waste, lonely.*
lee-lang, *live-long.*
lee, *shelter, peace;* set at little lee, 101, *left little peace?* "*left scarcely any means of shelter.*" JAMIESON.
leeze me on, 90, *I take pleasure or comfort in.*
lerrum, (Fr.) *leave.*
les, *lying.*
let, 278, *ceased.*
leugh, *laughed.*
levedy, *lady.*
libbe, *live.*
lidder, *lazy.*
lidder fat, *fat from laziness;* (qu. same as leeper fat?)
lightly, *make light of, treat with contempt.*
limmer, *rascal, scoundrelly.*
Lincome, *Lincoln;* Lincum twine, *Lincoln manufacture.*
ling, *heath.*
loan, *a piece of ground near a farm house where the cows are milked.*
loot, *let.*
lordswyk, *traitor to his lord.*
lore, loren, *lost.*
loudly, 124, *loud.*
loup, *leap, waterfall.*
louped, loupen, *leapt.*
lourd, *liefer, rather.*
low, *flame.*
lowne, *loon.*
luid, *loved.*
lyan, *lain.*
lyart, *hoary.*
lyke-wake, *watching of a dead body.*
lyves man, 271, *living man.*

ma, shame a, 93, *devil a bit.*
mae, *more.*
maill, *rent.*
mane, *moan.*
maries, *maids.*
marrows, *equals.*
maun, *must.*
may, *maid.*

me, *they* (Fr. *on*).
mear, *mare.*
mene, *moan.*
mergh, *marrow.*
mest, *most.*
minnie, *mother.*
mirk, *dark.*
modi, *bold.*
mot, *may.*
mounde, 270, *might?*
mowe, *may.*
mowes, *jests.*
mudie, *bold.*
muss, *moss.*

naggs, *notches.*
nede, 280, *he had not.*
neist, *next.*
nes, *was not.*
neuk, 224, *corner?*
nicher, nicker, *neigh.*
nie, *neigh.*
niest, *next.*
nogs, *stakes.*
noisome, 139, *annoying, vexatious.*
nolden, *would not.*
nome, *name.*
nome, nomen, *took.*
nones, *no.*
notour, 267, *notorious.*
noud, nout, *nought, not.*
nowt, *cattle.*
nule, *will not.*
nythe, 275, *wickedness.*

oht, *oath.*
onde, 275, *malice, envy.*
other, *or.*
ou, *you.*
ouir, *our.*
our, oure, *over.*
outspeckle, *laughing-stock.*
ower-word, *burden.*
owsen, *oxen.*

palliones, *tents.*
paw, neer play'd, 84, *did not stir hand or foot.*
peel, 106, *the stronghold, where the cattle were kept.*
pellettes, *balls.*
peruenke, *periwinkle.*
pestelets, *pistols, fire-arms.*
pleugh, *plough.*
plumet, 75, *pommel.*
poer, *power.*
pouraille, *common people.*
pris, 276, *praise.*
prude, *pride.*
prye, *pray.*
pure, *poor.*
putfalle, *pitfall.*
pyne, *pain.*

questry, *jury.*
quey, *young cow.*
quhavir, *whoever.*
quhilk, *which.*

rack, *a shallow ford, extending to a considerable breadth before it narrows into a full stream.* Jamieson.
rad, 27, *afraid.*
rae, *roe.*
raid, *foray, predatory incursion, fight.*

rank'd, 25, i. e. *looked finely, formed in ranks.*
ranshackled, *ransacked.*
rantin', *gay, jovial.*
rathere, 274, *sooner, beforehand.*
raxed, *stretched.*
ray, 102, *path* or *track.*
reaving, *robbing.*
redd, rede, *advise, advice.*
reek, *smoke.*
reif, *bailiff.*
reif, *robbery;* reiver, *robber.*
reil, reel.
remuy, *remove.*
res, 276, (Ang. Sax. *raes,*) *incursions, exploits?*
retheres hude, *bullock's hide.*
rig, 119, *ridge.*
rigging, *ridge, top.*
rin, *run.*
rok, *distaff.*
roof-tree, *the beam which forms the angle of the roof.*
rouncyn, *horse.*
routing, *bellowing.*
row, *roll.*
row-footed, 63, *rough-footed?*
rudds, *reddens.*
rude, *rood.*
Rumary, 249?
rybaus, *ribalds, villains.*

saft, 65, *light.*
saht, 276, *at one, reconciled.*
sark, *shirt, shift.*
saugh, *willow.*
sawe, *speech.*
schaw, *wood.*
scroggs, *stunted trees.*
see, *protect.*
see, 277, *seat, throne.*
seen, *soon.*
seld, *sold.*
selkethe, *strange.*
serime, 248, corrupt: qy. *betime?*
seth the, *after.*
served, 25, *behaved to.*
shame a ma, 93, *devil a bit.*
sheen, *shoes.*
sheil, *shepherd's hut.*
shome, *shame.*
shonde, *disgrace.*
shonkes, *shanks.*
sic, sicken, *such.*
skaithd, *injured.*
skeigh, *sky.*
slack, *a shallow dell, morass.*
slae, 119, *sloe.*
sleuth-dog, *blood-hound.*
slogan, *the gathering word peculiar to a family or clan, a war-cry.*
sloken, *slake.*
slough-hounds, *blood-hounds.*
slowen, *slew.*
smoldereth, *smothereth.*
snear, *snort.*
so, *as.*
solas, *amusement.*
sonde, godes, *God's sending.*
sote, *soot.*
soth, soht, *truth.*
Soudron, *Southerner, English.*
sould, suld, *should.*
sowie, *sow* (Lat. *vinea, pluteus*), *a shed or pent-house*

under cover of which the walls of a besieged town were assailed.
soy, *silk.*
spaits, *floods, torrents.*
spauld, *shoulder.*
spene, 272, *cost.*
spier, *ask.*
spin, *run.*
splent, *armor.*
springald, *a military engine for discharging heavy missiles at the walls of a beleaguered town.*
spuilye, spulzie, *despoil.*
star, see *ayeyn.*
starkest, *strongest.*
staun, *stolen.*
steads, *places.*
stear, *stir.*
stont, *stands.*
stots, *bullocks.*
stounde, *time.*
stour, *turmoil, affray.*
straught, *stretched.*
streynthe, *strength.*
strick, *strict.*
strinkled, *sprinkled.*
Strivelyn, *Sterling.*
stude, *place.*
sturt, 138, *trouble, disturbance.*
suereth, *swear.*
sugge, *say.*
suithe, *very.*
sunne, *sin.*
sweynes, 272, *swains, men in general below the rank of knights.*
swithe, *very.*
swither, *doubt, consternation.*
swyers, *squires.*
swykedom, *treachery.*
swythe, *very.*
syke, *ditch.*
syne, *then.*

tackles, *arrows.*
tald, *told.*
targats, 49, *tassels.*
te, *to.*
temed, 276, *tamed.*
thae, *these.*
thah, *though.*
the, *thrive.*
then, *than.*
thenche, *think*
theynes, *thanes.*
thir, *these;* thir's, *these are.*
this, *these.*
tho, *then.*
thole, *bear, endure.*
thonkes, his, 283, *willingly, gladly, by his good will.*
thrawin, 219, *distorted, wrinkled.*
thunche, 273, *seem.*
til, *to;* til't, *to it.*
tint, *lost.*
to-drawe, to-drowe, *drawn.*
to-dryven, 270, *break to pieces.*
token, 277, *gave to.*
tome, *tame.*
toom, *empty.*
tour, 192, *course or road.*
tow, 158, *throw.*
tprot, *interjection of contempt.*
trayne, *stratagem.*
tree, *staff.*

trepan'd, 180, *foully dealt with.*
trew, *trust.*
tryst, *meeting.*
tu-brugge, *draw-bridge.*
tul, *to.*
twa-fald, 15, *two-fold*, i. e. *with his body hanging down both sides.*
twa-some, *couple.*
twined, *parted.*

uch, *each.*
unkensome, *not to be recognized.*
unthought lang, hold, *keep from growing weary.*
upgive, 34, *acknowledge.*

villiche, *vilely.*
vor, *for.*
Vrenshe, *French.*
vyhte, *fighting.*
vylté, *disgrace.*

wad, *would.*
wad, 225, *wager, forfeit.*
Waleis, *Wallace.*
wally fa', 262, *ill luck befall.*
wan, *pale, dark, black.*
wan, *reached.*
wap, *tie round.*
waran, *guaranty.*
ware, 111, *lay out, use.*
ware, 272, (Ang. S. were, *capitis æstimatio*) *ransom, life-money.*
wark, *work.*
warrand, *protection.*
wat, *know.*
wat, *wet.*
waur, *worse.*
way, to the, 262, *away?*
wear, *guard.*
webbes, *weavers.*
wed, 247, qy. corrupt?
weht, *what.*
weel-fared, *well-favored.*
weil, 92, *eddy.*
weir, *war.*
wel the felle, 273, *will fall from thy head?*
wende, *weened.*
wes, *was.*
wesleyn, *western.*
wether, *whither.*
weylaway, *well-a-day!*
whang, *thong.*
whidderan, *whizzing.*
whet, *what.*
whew, *whistle.*
whosé, *any one whatever.*
wicker, 119, *switch.*
widdifu, *one who deserves to fill a widdie or halter, gallows bird, ruffian.*
wight, *strong, quick;* wightmen (Ang. Sax. wigman) *fighting men, brave fellows;* waled wightmen, 220, *picked warriors.*
win, *get.*
winna, *will not.*
winsomely, *handsomely.*
wit, *knowledge.*
wod, *waded.*
wombe, *belly.*
won, 120, misprint for win?
wons, *dwells.*

wood, *mad.*
worries, *strangles.*
Wudspurs, *Madspur*, *Hotspur.*
wyht, *wight.*
wysloker, *more wisely.*
wyte, *know.*
wyte, 282, *wait, watch* (?)

y, *in.*
yate, *gate.*
ybate, 280?
y-be, *been.*
y-brend, *burnt.*
y-caht, *caught.*
y-core, *chosen.*
y-cud, *known.*
y-demed, *judged.*
y-dyht, 278, *arranged.*
yeate, *gate.*
yef, *if.*
yeme, *govern.*
yere, to, 276, *this year.*
yestreen, *yesterday.*
yett, *gate.*
y-herde, *heard.*
y-knawe, *recognize.*
y-laht, *caught, taken.*
y-nemned, *named.*
yongeth, *goeth.*
y-suore, *sworn.*
y-tuht, *drawn.*
yynge, *young.*

zour, &c., *your*, &c.

www.ingramcontent.com/pod-product-compliance
Lightning Source LLC
LaVergne TN
LVHW022039110826
845151LV00007B/1034

* 9 7 8 1 4 2 5 5 2 8 9 2 8 *